THE RELATIONSHIP HANDBOOK

A Simple Guide To Satisfying Relationships

By George S. Pransky, PhD

25th Anniversary Edition

Published by
Pransky and Associates, P.S.
P.O. Box 498
La Conner, WA 98257
www.pranskyandassociates.com

(formerly published by TAB Books
a division of McGraw-Hill, Inc.)

© 2017 by **George Pransky**
Published by Pransky and Associates

Printed in the United States of America. All rights reserved. The publisher takes no responsibility for the use of any of the materials or methods described in this book, nor for products thereof.

ISBN 978-0-9988742-0-3

(Also published under the title Divorce Is Not the Answer: A Change of Heart Will Save Your Marriage, ISBN 0-8306-3583-1.)

The Library of Congress has cataloged the second edition as follows:

Pransky, George
The relationship handbook: a simple guide to more satisfying relationships/by George S. Pransky
p. Cm
Includes bibliographical references and index.
ISBN: 0-9711988-0-2 (p)
1. Marriage-United States. 2. Interpersonal relations.
3. Communications in marriage-United States.
I.Title.
HQ734.P838 2001
646'8-dc20
Library of Congress Control Number: 2001093984

25th Anniversary Edition

DEDICATION

I dedicate this book to my wife Linda. Her inspiration and encouragement made this book possible. Her love and companionship woke me up to the possibilities that exist in marriage.

ACKNOWLEDGMENTS

Sydney Banks inspired the understanding that was worth writing about. I also owe a great debt to every couple I have ever counseled. You educated me on where the rubber meets the road in day-to-day relationship life. You taught me exactly what to address in *The Relationship Handbook* that would help people the most.

I couldn't possibly give Linda, my wife and business partner, enough acknowledgment for the role she played in the creation of *The Relationship Handbook*. You might even say that *The Relationship Handbook* is *our* relationship story. What you'll find within its pages is the wisdom that brought us together, that kept us together and that still benefits the two of us to this day.

Thank you to Bailey Cunningham for her work as editor of the 25th Anniversary Edition. Thank you, also, to Véronique Pivetta for coordinating the translated versions. Her work made it possible for this book to reach readers across the globe. And finally, thank you to the incredible translators whose names can be found under 'Credits'.

CONTENTS

Dedication	3
Acknowledgments	3
Preface—How My Marriage Was Saved	7
The Power of a Change of Heart	10
1 A Fresh Start	13
2 Compatibility Is Only a Thought Away	21
3 Communication—When You Need It, It Won't Work	35
4 Moods—The Key to Understanding People	42
5 Emotions—Master or Servant?	54
6 Compassion or Resentment?—The Choice Is Yours	67
7 Dissatisfaction—A Mental Illness	77
8 Effortless, Permanent Change—Possibility or Pipe Dream?	87
9 Bringing out the Best in People	99
10 Don't Deal with Problems—Transcend Them	116
11 The Source of Conflict—No One Will Ever See the World You See	131
12 Exit Excitement, Enter Love—Levels of Relationships	143
13 It's Never Too Late to Get a Fresh Start	159

14 Intimacy—Plain and Simple	175
15 Commitment—Self-Sacrifice or Self-Serving?	183
16 Summary	190

Addendum—25 Years Later

Preface	195
1 Introduction—Where It All Began	197
2 The Three Principles—The Cure for Relationship Failure	202
3 Getting over Yourself—Why You Need to Do It	208
4 Productive Conversations—How to Make It Happen	215
5 Good Listening—The Overlooked Relationship Skill	224
6 Can You Be Happy With Anyone?	230
7 Final Thoughts	239
Additional Resources	241
Credits	243

PREFACE
HOW MY MARRIAGE WAS SAVED

During the first three years of our relationship, my wife and I struggled. We argued, we tried to change each other and we tried to compromise. We made agreements, and we communicated fully. Nothing worked. It seemed the more we "worked" on our relationship, the farther apart we grew.

We got discouraged. We went to counselors and friends, only to find they were struggling with these same problems.

We were in the helping profession, presenting seminars for professionals and the public on communication and awareness skills, yet all the latest technology of the human potential movement in California in the 1970s could not keep our own relationship afloat.

Fortunately for us, we met someone who woke us up about relationships. This man was theosopher/author Syd Banks. [1] The first time we saw Syd, he was speaking in a large meeting room. In the audience there were at least ten happy couples. Ten happy couples were more happy couples than we had seen in our lives!

After the meeting, we talked with some of these couples. They were very intimate and relaxed. It was obvious that they

---

[1] Syd Banks is the author of *Second Chance* and *In Quest of the Pearl* (Surfside Publishing, A Division of Duval-Bibb Publishing Co., Florida, 1989).

enjoyed themselves and each other. They said all the couples there had a history of conflict that had turned around when they began listening to Syd.

We went to the next talk and this time we really listened. Syd suggested that positivity and understanding were the keys to successful relationships. He said through happiness, the so-called "problems" of your relationship would take care of themselves.

I was convinced, however, that if Syd knew our relationship, he would consider us an exception to what he was espousing. Yet I could see his message was helping people. Maybe what he was saying would help us.

It did. We eased off trying to change each other. We began to enjoy and appreciate each other. This became a way of life, and our old habit of struggling fell away. Our relationship turned around from continually getting worse despite our efforts, to continuously improving without the need of our efforts. This book is inspired by our turnaround. If it could happen for us, it could happen to any relationship. All it took was *understanding*. The understanding that helped us is spelled out in this book.

When couples come in for counseling they don't really want to learn how to cope. They want an easy, satisfying relationship. Coping, struggling and compromise have appeal only in a world that has lost sight of effortless, harmonious relationships. Unfortunately, this is such a world. The understanding level in relationships is so low that struggle, coping and divorce are the norm. The current thinking about relationships is laden with myths that lead people toward marital discord.

This book speaks to thirteen of the most prevalent and misleading myths. A more productive view of relationships is offered as an alternative to each myth. Case studies and other support materials illustrate the myths and their alternatives.

Our clinical experience has taught us which relationship issues are most difficult for people. This book could properly be subtitled "The ideas, metaphors and vignettes that have proven most useful to the clients we have helped."

One editor of my manuscript suggested I tone down the case studies. He felt they had "unrealistically" happy endings. The case studies are based on actual clinical cases. The clients' responses are real. If you think these responses are "unrealistic", you are selling the human race short. One purpose of this book is to raise readers' vision of how quickly and dramatically people can change—to give the reader a more "realistic" view of people.

The case studies in this book are not verbatim, however; they are distillations of actual cases. So, one "session" in the text might represent several clinical sessions.

If you read this book with an open mind you will see there is an easy way to be together in a relationship. Maybe someday a child will ask, "Why were there so many unhappy marriages back in the 1990s and before?" Her parent might respond: "I don't really know. I guess people just didn't understand relationships in those days. I'm so glad we have this understanding now."

THE POWER OF A CHANGE OF HEART

This book is a change-of-heart facilitator. If you have a change of heart, your marriage will be on a new footing. A change of heart is the almost magical force that erases the distress in relationships and gives you a fresh start.

If you have a physical dysfunction—a bad kidney, broken leg or an ulcer—it takes time to recover. Only in the worst case is the damage irreversible. In contrast, a relationship dysfunction—a conflict, boredom or resentment—needs no healing time and is always reversible. A change of heart can occur in an instant.

I know a change of heart heals relationships. This book will show you what a change of heart is, how natural it is and how completely it cures us. If people understood the accessibility and power of a change of heart, divorce would be an oddity and marriage counselors would serve as change-of-heart agents.

There are many books out about relationships, as well as many marriage counselors working to help couples. Why is the divorce rate so high and why are happy marriages so rare?

Every field has had a period during which unsound practices were observed, and then superseded by new understandings. When I was a kid, my parents insisted I eat high-cholesterol foods such as eggs, red meat and dairy products. Now people know these foods present health hazards. Before an understanding of germ theory, people drank water contaminated by sewage and passed on communicable diseases. Today, sound sanitation practices arrest the spread of infectious disease.

At least since the 1960s, the field of relationship counseling has been in the dark about what makes relationships dysfunctional and what cures them. So, the public and counselors alike innocently have been throwing gasoline on the fires of marital discord in an attempt to quench them.

The understanding presented in this book provides the "water" to douse these fires and keep them out. I know this understanding works because I have seen myriad relationships turn around in my years of clinical practice. This understanding is not new. It is common sense that has been lost in the misinformation innocently proliferated by the field of psychology.

Someday this book may seem a crude expression of this understanding. As it joins the mainstream, the understanding will be refined and developed, just as germ and nutrition theory have evolved over time. Today, this book represents a 180-degree departure from current relationship theory—and a philosophy that offers hope where none existed before.

Many marriage counselors say the past—its unexpressed emotions and habit patterns—and poor communication are the "bad guys" that cause mental and relationship distress. These are the symptoms of relationship distress, not the cause. The cause, the real bad guy, is insecurity. Painful memories, negative emotions, habit patterns and bad communication are all symptoms of insecurity.

If you want to understand why people do as they do and feel the way they feel, you need only understand the role of insecurity in life. Insecurity is the source of distress and all counterproductive behavior. Thoughts of insecurity periodically pass through our minds. If we dismiss these thoughts, we will remain secure, our ideal selves: easygoing, joyful, compassionate and wise. If we harbor our thoughts of insecurity, we end up in a state of distress.

Insecurity is the generic human mental illness. The cure is to understand the psychological forces of thought, feelings and states of mind. This book explains how these forces provide joy and satisfaction in life and in relationships.

1
A FRESH START

Couples who go to marriage counseling often separate. Counselors contend that this makes sense because the marriages were troubled to start with. A better explanation is that most marriage counseling doesn't work because:

- Therapists tend to teach couples to struggle with their problems instead of giving them a fresh start.
- Therapists use low mood therapy instead of high mood therapy.
- Clients are given misinformation, the same misinformation that explains why so many therapists get divorced.

When couples go to a marriage counselor there are three possible outcomes: (1) they get a fresh start, (2) they stay together and "cope with" a tense or sour marriage, or (3) they separate. Every couple wants the first outcome. They want to have a fresh start and be happy together. If they can't get a fresh start, they will jump to the third choice—separation—because they don't want the second. They have already been coping and are tired of it.

Coping involves struggling (a more honest term for "working on") with problems and expressing your feeling about them. Coping takes time and work and provides only temporary relief. It is about as effective as releasing steam without turning down the heat. Eventually, expending all that energy wears the couple down and leads to discouragement and divorce.

Problems and adversity are not the crux of marital discord. All couples face adversity, but it doesn't cause problems for harmonious couples. Couples with satisfying marriages don't "cope" with their lives and with each other. They don't work on their marriages. The strength of their marriages lies not in their ability to cope with their problems, but in their ability to keep their bearings and to stay close. This book shows couples how to do that.

MISINFORMATION ABOUT RELATIONSHIPS

Before today's consciousness about cholesterol, people were encouraged to eat fatty foods, which we now know contribute to a high rate of heart disease. Similarly, today's misinformation about relationships has led to a high divorce rate and a generally low level of satisfaction among couples who manage to stay together.

People mistakenly believe that pain and effort are an inevitable part of relationships. They believe that analyzing their problems and living patterns will change them. Analyzing problems makes you an expert on your problems. It doesn't change you. When partners probe and analyze each other's faults, as they learn to do in most marriage counseling, they become insecure, defensive and resistant to change. They bring out the worst in each other.

LOW MOOD THERAPY

Few couples know that there are actually two kinds of therapy: low mood therapy and high mood therapy. During low mood therapy the client is in a low mood because he's probing problems and other negative thoughts. In high mood therapy, clients engage the thoughts we have in high moods—insights, non-contingent positive feelings and big-picture perspectives.

Why does low mood therapy exist? Because the therapist sees her job as helping troubled people, it makes sense to her to be sitting opposite a troubled person. She sees the discouragement in her clients but believes it's appropriate because their problems are so formidable. The therapist believes that problems and issues cause marital discord. She doesn't realize they are merely symptoms.

Let's say the counselor worked with three couples today and has been in a low mood with them. The fourth couple arrives in a high mood, in a good position to listen and learn. Unfortunately, the counselor's low mood is likely to bring them down. The pain of doing low mood therapy is contagious.

Low mood therapists are dedicated professionals. They are so dedicated they are even willing to feel down in order to do their jobs. The burnout for low mood therapists comes fast—often in four or five years. If they knew that keeping themselves and their clients in a low mood was counterproductive, they would surely do things differently.

THE LOW MOOD THERAPY PROCESS

1. The counselor asks clients to list their problems. This step makes all the problems vivid in the clients' minds, thereby lowering their spirits.

2. Counselor and clients delve into each problem in detail. They look at its cause, its implications and associated memories, emotions and fears. Problems now seem so formidable that clients are discouraged.

3. From this discouraged state of mind, the counselor and clients attempt to solve relationship problems. The process is usually painful and unproductive.

4. The counselor concludes that the couple needs to put extensive "work" into their relationship. He or she then asks if they are willing to make the commitment. The couple considers how painful and unproductive their efforts have been and are reluctant to throw "good money after bad."

You will notice there is a downward progression in these four steps. Each step lowers the mood farther. As the clients' spirits plummet, the problems seem more difficult and therapy becomes less productive.

HIGH MOOD THERAPY

The high mood therapist sees that extracting misunderstandings, misinformation, overreactions, grudges and discouragement from relationships lays a foundation for a fresh start. This observation keeps the high mood therapist hopeful and patient.

She doesn't focus on problems. Instead, she explains personality and mood distortions and shows how misinformation damages relationships. Once this understanding strikes home, the couple begins to glimpse the same possibilities for their relationship that the therapist sees. They see the viability of a fresh start. At this point, the couple sees their relationship history as a nightmare from which they are awakening.

Here is an example of high mood therapy in action:

> Jennifer and Ben have been living in harmony for more than six months. One morning Jennifer

wakes up in an extremely low mood. Each person has a unique way of acting out moods; Jennifer's is to be critical. She criticizes Ben for working too much and doing too little housework. He is dismayed. He doesn't realize it is Jennifer's low mood talking, not Jennifer.

Ben gets insecure about the relationship, and his mood drops. His way of acting out his low mood is to withdraw. Ben's insecurity and withdrawal frighten Jennifer, and her mood drops lower. She becomes critical of his distance and demands more contact with him. Feeling attacked, Ben withdraws farther. The spiral continues.

A characteristic of very low moods is that every little problem looks like the tip of an iceberg. Ben and Jennifer begin to question whether they are right for each other. In the ignorance of low moods, they think the "real" Ben and Jennifer have finally surfaced. They don't understand what has happened and so they believe their thoughts. They keep remembering the incident and are afraid it will happen again. They are now locked in a fearful, cautious mind-set. Their relationship is punctuated by insecurity, their mood held down by their fearful thoughts.

They bring their problem to a high mood therapist. Instead of analyzing their pattern of criticism and withdrawal, she reassures them that they have innocently brought out the worst in each other. She shows them that their behaviors have become exaggerated because they have been stuck in a low mood. She explains how moods distort our thinking and perceptions. She explains that if they make allowances for them, moods will have no lasting effect on relationships.

Ben and Jennifer see that the therapist is sincere and caring, and notice that she is hopeful despite their concerns. Her optimism is contagious. They can see how what they learned about moods will help them and they are excited about learning more.

Moods are the constant shifts in perspective built into our experience of life. Our thinking and therefore our perceptions of life are a function of mood changes. Our thoughts are more optimistic, lighthearted, and wise when we are in a high mood.

This understanding of moods is only one contribution that the high mood therapist makes to clients. There are other building blocks to support a maintenance-free, harmonious relationship.

This book emphasizes thinking because it is the steering wheel for a happy life and satisfying relationships. Thinking is like breathing—we do it continuously from birth to death. Thinking is like a function that allows every human being to create a personal reality. Each thought creates a feeling that makes the thought appear real. If we think we are old, for example, we suddenly feel old. If we think our "to do lists" are overwhelming, we will feel overwhelmed and stressed. We can easily be fooled into thinking the feeling of stress was caused by the list itself rather than our thoughts about it.

There is no way to enjoy a relationship if our minds are full of painful thoughts. We can't enjoy anything while our minds are analyzing and criticizing. Troubled spouses report their spirits start dropping when they even think of going home. Yet, they don't recognize the tricks their thoughts are playing on them. As our thought processes get healthier, more responsive (less habitual), our relationships improve dramatically. High mood therapy provides the software for healthy thinking.

What makes people so rigid, so predictable in their thinking? Mind-sets, which we also could call thought systems, create unique realities for people in the same way a film creates an image on a movie screen. A mind-set predisposes us toward specific feelings and behaviors. Mind-sets limit our perceived options and, in that way, cast our lot in life. We change our lot as we understand mind-sets and make allowances for them. When we don't know mind-sets exist, we have conflicts with each other. When we do, we can navigate individual differences gracefully.

Often people think of feelings as things to work through or deal with. But feelings were meant to be a barometer to help us maintain our emotional equilibrium. Feelings provide our moment-to-moment experience of life. They tell us the extent to which our perceptions are distorted by our moods and thought systems.

THE HIGH MOOD THERAPY PROCESS

1. The counselor finds and fans any spark of intimacy that exists between the partners. The couple begins to feel closer to each other and more hopeful about the relationship.

2. The counselor describes how insecurity distorts behavior in relationships. He or she suggests that the relationship is not in as bad shape as it seems. The clients begin to see the spiral of emotional reactions that destroyed the closeness they want. They begin to see innocence in themselves and each other.

3. The counselor demonstrates that maintaining a sense of well-being is all it takes to make the relationship enjoyable and easy.

4. The counselor teaches them the building blocks of human psychological functioning: thinking, moods, mind-sets and feelings. Understanding these principles enables the couple to create and maintain a sense of well-being and to feel warm and respectful toward each other, even in hard times.

5. According to the couple's needs, the counselor discusses relationship-related subjects such as what the past really is, how to forgive and forget, how to use feeling as a compass of relationship well-being and how compatibility is the result of the feeling, not the cause.

To get a fresh start in a marriage, we must know that the so-called "issues" in a marriage are symptoms and not causes of disharmony. The cause of marital problems is bad software, a misunderstanding of the deeper dynamics of a relationship.

The ultimate purpose of this book is to move the reader toward living in a state of healthy psychological functioning. Two people living in this state will have a stable relationship. In a healthy state we are like Dr. Jekyll. When we lose this state, hello Mr. Hyde. Mr. and Mrs. Jekyll always have a good marriage. Mr. and Mrs. Hyde always have problems. It takes only one Jekyll to move a marriage towards health.

This book helps couples bring out the best in each other. I will show you how well-being fosters healthy behavior. Each chapter exposes a popular, but destructive, misconception about relationships and provides a new understanding that can give troubled couples the fresh start they need.

2
COMPATIBILITY IS ONLY A THOUGHT AWAY

"We're just too different. At least he is."

"We're just too different. We're incompatible." That's what almost every client says at some point. The truth is, there is no such thing as "too different." This chapter discloses how differences fit within relationships. It explains that compatibility has to do with how you think and feel and not with how different you are. If you catch on, you won't have to go to counseling to deal with incompatibility because it's an illusion.

THE COMPATIBILITY MYTH

Don't personalities have to be compatible for a marriage to be successful?

THE GRAIN OF TRUTH

A couple must feel compatible and close for a marriage to work.

THE CHANGE OF HEART

> "Jack Spratt could eat no fat;
> His wife could eat no lean;
> So 'twixt them both they cleared the cloth,
> And licked the platter clean."

The Spratts' food preferences can be viewed from two perspectives. From one perspective Mrs. Spratt would say, "Jack and I are completely incompatible. We can't even agree on what cut of meat to get from the butcher." From the other, she'd say, "Jack and I complement each other perfectly. Any piece of meat satisfies us both."

Complementary and incompatible are two conclusions about the same situation, two sides of the same coin. When differences are viewed with respect, partners are viewed as complementary. The same differences viewed from a feeling of discontent will make the partners seem incompatible. It is the feeling that makes the difference.

Respect and affinity are the feelings that turn the personality differences into assets in a relationship. These feelings allow one person to learn from another. For example, let's say an outgoing woman is married to a quiet, reserved man. If this couple has the right feelings for each other, each will learn from the other rather than attempt to remake the other person in his or her image. She will learn to be easily satisfied and he will pick up on her social graces. Each will be grateful for the balance the other person adds to the relationship.

Thoughts of incompatibility are a sign that the respect and affinity level in the relationship has slipped. It is always humbling to realize that today's incompatibility was yesterday's "refreshing difference." The two perspectives are just one thought apart.

The following chart shows how the same behavior leads to different interpretations when one is predisposed to either a negative or positive feeling:

Objective Behavior	Viewed from a *negative* predisposition	Viewed from a *positive* predisposition
Youthful	childish	childlike
Trusts that life is as it appears to be	gullible, naïve	innocent
Holds a position despite resistance	stubborn	committed
Readily offers comments	opinionated	outspoken
Frequently asks for what she wants	aggressive	assertive
Tends to notice the positive side of life	unrealistic	optimistic

HOW THOUGHT CREATES INCOMPATIBILITY

We all have accumulated mental images of what we want in a marriage: a mate who is handy around the house, a mate with exceptional social graces, a mate who likes drives in the country, a mate who is a homebody, a mate who is a social live-wire and so on. We think we want different things from a marriage, but we really all want the same things: to be close to our mates and enjoy their company. Closeness, a warm feeling of affinity, is the cake and the frosting.

Even dissimilar values and economic incompatibility don't matter if the emotional connection is there. Warm feelings give people a positive outlook. If, for example, two people with a good feeling between them don't agree on finances, they won't be bothered by this "incompatibility." Their good feelings insulate them in the following ways:

- Their focus will be off the money issue because it will be on enjoying the intimacy they share.

- When they do notice their differences in this area, they will consider them to be "interesting" or "cute."

- If their differences did stall a financial decision, each would see the stalemate as a golden opportunity to do a nice thing for the other.

- Any momentary friction they felt would remind them how little friction they have in their relationship. The friction would disappear in a wave of gratitude.

It is only when we lose good feelings that the qualities we think we want in a mate become important to us. In fact, the number and strength of our wants is an excellent indicator of relationship well-being. When we start to feel we are not getting what we want in our marriage, we know our level of intimacy is low.

Being close helps us to get the things we want, such as a good sexual relationship or material luxury, because intimacy leads to good teamwork. Closeness brings out the best in each person. It also inspires both partners to attend to the things that are important to their mates, making it easier to realize their joint and individual goals.

HOW DIFFERENT CAN BE COMPATIBLE

In many states, "irreconcilable differences" is grounds for divorce. Which of the following determines how simple differences become irreconcilable differences?

    A. The nature of the differences

    B. The size of the differences

    C. The number of differences

    D. ALL of the above

    E. NONE of the above

"E" is the correct answer. The issue is never the size, number or even in the nature of the differences. The determining factor will always be whether you think these differences are important. Once you think they are, you may use their size, number or nature to justify the conclusion of incompatibility.

It is the thought of incompatibility that creates the feeling of incompatibility. History provides every possible extreme of incompatibility within successful unions. Many marriages have survived in the face of daunting taboos. Daughters and sons of warring chieftains have tied the knot and thrived. Missionaries who live in separate countries have enjoyed loving, enduring marriages. We have all, sometime, been surprised by an unlikely couple who found marital bliss.

Let's look at an example. A woman told a marriage therapist that her husband was in jail and had served five years of a ten-year sentence. She said she visited him every day. The therapist thought he knew what was coming. He expected her to be ambivalent about remaining married or resentful about how much she was giving and how little she was getting back. To his amazement her problem was just the opposite.

"I came in to see if I'm crazy," she said to him. "I feel a lot of love for my husband. I carry him in my heart all day long. I am grateful to be married to such a man. Of course, I wish he were out of prison so that we could live together."

"It's good you love your husband. Why are you concerned about that?" replied the therapist.

"My friends tell me I should divorce him and get another husband. They say it's wrong to be satisfied with my situation."

"Are your friends happy in their marriages?"

"Not really. They don't like the way they are treated. They don't seem to appreciate their marriages. Only one of my friends is happily married. Come to think of it, she is the only one who seems to approve of my feelings."

"The point of marriage is to have the feelings you and your husband share," he said. "Yes, it would be better to have companionship, too, but having those feelings in your heart is the most important thing."

The client was relieved. She knew she felt happy and in love with her husband. She had entertained the idea that they would have to divorce. It was a relief to hear the definition of compatibility that related to inside feelings rather than the external situation.

Suppose a wife is loud, opinionated, plays golf incessantly and likes weird movies, but her husband doesn't resent these traits. Would he feel compatible with his wife? Of course he would.

There really is no such thing as incompatibility. It is all in our minds. Were this not the case, there wouldn't be such an unlikely assortment of happy couples in the world.

Compatibility is a product of thought, a figment of the imagination. If we think a characteristic is incompatible, then we will get a negative feeling from that thought. The negative feeling is what we call "incompatibility." Were we to have a change of heart and think of the characteristic as good or unimportant, we would feel compatible again.

Compatibility is a matter of the heart. True compatibility is sharing a positive feeling. It is enjoying the time you spend together.

By nature, all human beings are compatible in that people simply like being with other people, no matter what the activity. We all know the experience of doing something "boring" with a friend, yet having a good time. The company put us in the frame of mind to enjoy it.

This natural compatibility is upset by negative thoughts and judgments. If I am with a person and I entertain negative thoughts about how that person lives or is, my positive feelings begin to disappear. The feeling of compatibility in a relationship will diminish when one person is troubled by thoughts about the other.

THINKING TURNS PRINCES INTO FROGS

A couple looks at their differences and feels bad about their marriage. It is not the differences that make them feel bad. It is the negative feeling that accompanies the act of looking at those differences. The practice of analysis, self-doubt and faultfinding muddies your view of relationships and makes frogs out of princes.

The list below shows how the labels we assign to personal differences and our conclusions about them reflect varying levels of understanding our thoughts. The case involves a socially inclined woman with a homebody husband.

↓ Toward Compatibility	
Intolerable	What's the sense of having a mate if he won't do things with you?
A problem	We can't stay home and go out at the same time.
Irritating	He never wants to go anywhere.
Acceptable	Couples are bound to have some differences.
Interesting	I wonder what he likes so much about being a homebody. I would get bored staying at home.
Synergy	He's teaching me to enjoy the simple pleasures of life.
Endearing	I love to see him enjoying himself puttering around the house.
☺	

When thoughts of incompatibility cross our minds, they signal that we are in a low mood. If we were in a high mood we would view differences from the positive end (☺) of the chart. In low moods, we would be thinking the statements from the negative end.

AN IMPASSE OVER HAVING CHILDREN [2]

Jim, 34, and Paula, 31, have been married for six years. Both were married previously; neither has any children. They came into counseling because they were at an impasse on the issue of having children. Jim wants to begin a family and Paula does not.

---

[2] Case studies are based on actual clinical cases. They are not verbatim, however; they are distillations. Consequently, one "session" in the text might represent several clinical sessions.

Jim. I don't see how we can stay married when we disagree on such an important issue.

Paula. But you knew how I felt when we got married.

Jim. I didn't care so much then, but I do now. I really want to have a family.

Paula. I'm telling you, Jim, I'm just not into it. I like my career and I *don't* want the responsibility of a child.

Therapist. I can see there's a lot of discomfort about having kids.

Jim. There has been for some time now.

Therapist. What about the times when you're not thinking about having children? Do you feel close then?

Paula. I suppose so. We drift in and out of being close, but this "kid problem" is taking up more of our energy and attention.

Therapist. You know, a lot of your thinking is affected by how close you are. Everyone is that way. When you're very close, you probably don't think as much about whether to have children. You tend to think more about each other. But when you begin to drift apart and feel a little lonely, you probably start thinking about having a family. Jim, am I right?

Jim. I don't know if it's that cut-and-dried, but I know that I do go in and out of thinking about having kids.

Therapist. Does your objection to having children get weaker or stronger at different times, Paula?

Paula. Well, I don't know—I guess I do fluctuate a lot. It's a little confusing. Why do my feelings change like that?

Therapist. Look at it this way. When people are insecure, what they want and don't want feels a lot more compelling to them. But when our spirits are high, we're more understanding. We can see both sides more easily. We see that "issues" are not as important in the grand scheme of things as we thought they were. In other words, it's normal for us to be stubborn when we're in a low mood and magnanimous when we're in a higher frame of mind.

Jim. C'mon, are you saying if I stayed in a good frame of mind I wouldn't want to have a family?

Therapist. No, you might still prefer that. But you wouldn't care as much. You would see having kids as frosting on the cake and not the cake itself.

Jim. Okay. So what's the cake then?

Therapist. The cake is feeling contented inside. In your marriage, the cake is sharing good feelings as a couple. But couples can lose sight of the closeness in their marriage when they search for the specific conditions they *think* they want. Often, the only reason they want those specific conditions is that they assume they will bring more love. For example, some couples work hard to accumulate money so that they can take great vacations and become closer someday. In pursuing that goal, they drift apart. Soon, each accuses the other of interfering with their joint plans. They lose sight of the original intent, which was feeling close.

Paula. How does that apply to us? We have no conflict about money.

Therapist. Let me spell it out. Couples have specific ideas and goals for what they want in their marriage: lifestyle, children, hobbies and so forth. They don't wish for these things as ends but rather as means to their happiness. They expect these goals will make them happier and bring them closer together.

Jim. Of course these things will bring more happiness.

Therapist. You would think these things would create at least some happiness. Often, they create distress instead. It is easy to get so focused, so involved, in the goal that we lose sight of the purpose behind the goal—to increase well-being and closeness. For example, a couple might improve their standard of living by sacrificing their mental health and the amount of time they spend together. They might work too much, become edgy with each other and ruin the good feeling between them. Are you with me so far?

Paula. Yes. I've seen that happen to some of our friends.

Therapist. Pursuing the goal actually takes the couple away from the closeness they desire. They have lost perspective on what really matters.

Jim. Are you saying that my desire to have children has been bad for the relationship?

Therapist. I'm saying that you have allowed your attitudes about the children issue to contaminate the relationship. Your thoughts about children have caused a strain between you instead of enhancing your feelings about each other.

Paula. You know, Jim, I have definitely been guilty of spoiling things between us that way. I've thought more about whether to have a child than I have about you. In some way, I guess I've been seeing you as a hassle I want to avoid.

Jim. What are we supposed to do, forget about having children?

Paula. No, we just have to be careful not to hurt each other's feelings over the children issue. We have to be more gentle with each other and more open. I have been so close-minded and harsh. I have acted as if the children issue is more important than the relationship between us.

Jim. I don't understand. Are you saying you want children now?

Paula. No. I'm saying our focus on having or not having children has smothered the feeling in our relationship. I mean, look, even right now I feel much warmer toward you. I appreciate what we have together. I lost sight of that with all the talking and thinking about having children.

Jim. I don't feel any different.

Therapist. You're still thinking about the children, right?

Jim. Yeah. I definitely want to get this issue resolved.

Therapist. I have a homework assignment for you two. It might sound crazy.

Paula. What is it?

Therapist. I want you just to enjoy each other in the two weeks before our next appointment. Forget the "child issue" as much as possible.

Jim. I can't believe I'm paying you to hear a suggestion like that.

Therapist. Believe it or not, Jim, taking focus off an issue and attending to the feeling between you is often the best way to move toward resolution.

Jim. I don't believe it but I'll *force* myself to enjoy Paula these two weeks, if you say so.

Two Weeks Later

Therapist. Well, how were your two weeks of enjoying each other?

Paula. I'd say we did pretty well at not thinking about "the issue." Actually, we were better than I thought we'd be. The more time that went by without discussing it, the easier it was to not think about it.

Therapist. How were your two weeks, Jim?

Jim. To tell you the truth, it was a relief not to discuss the problem. It reminded me of when we were first married. I looked forward to coming home. I must admit, though, I don't feel any more resolved about the issue. It's just that it isn't on my mind as much, and when it is on my mind, it doesn't bother me as much.

Paula. The same thing is true for me, now that you mention it. I don't feel as sensitive about it.

Therapist. That's a start. Once your analytical mind lets go of an issue, your internal wisdom has a chance to take over. Your thinking is freed up and can start to evolve.

Several Sessions Later

Paula. Now I'm really confused. This week I've been thinking it might be nice to have kids. I've been noticing babies all week.

Jim. Really? What changed your mind?

Paula. I don't know, I guess I feel closer to you now. We were so much into leading our own separate lives before, I imagined myself bringing up the child alone. I just feel maybe there's a positive side to having a child. I was looking at all the inconveniences. All I could see were my negative feelings. No wonder I was so against kids! I'm more open to it now, though. But I have to say I'm a little overwhelmed by the idea.

Therapist. It's common that someone fixated on an issue sees only a small part of it. When your perspective comes back, you see the big picture. It's only when you see the big picture that you realize what you saw before was only a fraction of it.

Jim. I'll have to admit I don't feel so sure any more either. I can see a lot of my desire to have a child was coming from my insecurity. I felt kind of empty inside and the idea of having a child appealed to me. I thought having a child would fill me up. I still like the idea of having a family but now I see there's a lot more to it. For one thing, I want Paula to want to have a child, too. It has to have her blessing too or it wouldn't be right. If she thinks it's too much work, we shouldn't do it.

Paula. It wouldn't be work to me if I was really into the idea. The fact you want a child means a lot to me.

Therapist. You don't have to decide right now in my office. Now that you two are open-minded, your thinking about having a family is bound to change with time. When having a child is in the cards for both of you, you'll know it.

IN A NUTSHELL

- Thoughts of compatibility or incompatibility are a compass that reacts to your level-of-closeness to the other person. When you are feeling close to your mate, you will entertain thoughts about how compatible you are.

- Remember that today's incompatibilities were yesterday's refreshing differences. Those differences represent opportunities to learn from each other. If you take the role of the student, the respect you show your mate will raise the level of the relationship.

3
COMMUNICATION
WHEN YOU NEED IT, IT WON'T WORK

"We must learn to communicate so we can find out just how bad things are."

Clients come into therapy thinking that communication does for a relationship what brushing and flossing do for our teeth. The truth is, communication enhances a relationship that is on track. If a relationship is off track, communication is, at best, like brushing your teeth right before you eat candy. At worst, communication is tantamount to brushing your teeth with a tooth brush dipped in plaque.

THE COMMUNICATION MYTH

Doesn't clear communication automatically improve the quality of a relationship?

THE GRAIN OF TRUTH

Positive communication does deepen the feeling between two people.

THE CHANGE OF HEART

The couple told the counselor they had a "communication problem." They said they had bad feelings toward each other. The counselor responded, "It's a good thing your communication is poor. Just think how terrible you'd feel if you could get your ill feelings across to each other." The counselor then helped the couple find a close, warm feeling in their relationship—he facilitated a *change of heart*. When they felt close, they saw the problem in their relationship was the feeling, not the communication.

Suppose you have a pipe that brings water to your house. Dirty, polluted water passes through the pipe into your water tank. Is that pipe improving the quality of the water that passes through it. Communication is a pipe through which feelings pass. If the feelings are positive, the relationship will be uplifted. If they are negative, the couple's level of closeness will drop.

In a relationship, then, the quality of feelings that passes through the communication pipe determines the state of that union. What brings new closeness and goodwill to a relationship is more positive feelings—not more talk. Good feelings are expressed in all kinds of ways besides talk. They radiate from your presence.

THE COMMUNICATION BANK

Say you have a relationship savings account. Its currency is feelings. Its balance is the level of goodwill that exists between you and your partner. Every interaction that comes from a feeling of goodwill or affinity is a deposit in the account. Every time you speak when you are feeling ill will, you are making a withdrawal. The stronger the feeling, the larger the transaction. This analogy shows how communication can enhance a relationship or bankrupt it. "If you can't say something nice, don't say anything at all," is part of the key to relationship riches, but not all. Feeling bad about someone and saying nothing withdraws from your relationship account. Conversely, having good thoughts about someone, even if unspoken, is a deposit.

I used to think that what you said when you were drunk was what you truly thought. I was wrong. What you say when you are drunk is what you think when you are drunk. Being drunk is a state of mind. Being angry is a state of mind. So is being happy. Each state of mind has its own special thoughts and feelings. When we communicate from drunkenness, anger or happiness, what we say can only be understood within the context of that state of mind.

If the two of you start a discussion at 7:10 P.M. and at 7:30 you feel closer, you are making progress. Your level of closeness is a moment-to-moment measure of your progress. There is no such thing as a productive discussion that alienates its parties. There is no such thing as an unproductive discussion that brings two people closer together.

THEY COULDN'T TALK TO EACH OTHER

Judy and Phil wanted to learn to communicate better. They have been married for eight years and have three young children. They came into counseling because they could not talk to each other without getting upset. They said their relationship had been difficult for six years. The therapist has just told them the problem is not their communication but the feeling they have for each other.

Judy. You're right. We don't feel too good about each other but that's because we can't communicate.

Therapist. Actually, Judy, communication takes care of itself. It's the feelings that need to be tended to. Is it accurate for me to assume you both feel upset and discouraged after you talk?

Judy. That's true. We invariably end that way.

Therapist. And you start out feeling upset and discouraged before the talk also. Isn't that true? (Judy and Phil both nod.)

Therapist. In that sense, your communication process is totally successful. It enables you to share the bad feelings you're focusing on. Communication is a neutral transport container; it carries whatever feelings you have.

Phil. But if we feel bad toward each other, shouldn't we express it?

Therapist. If you do express those feelings you risk making the other person feel just as bad about you.

Phil. I know what you mean. Sometimes I'm in pretty good spirits and we'll have a talk and bang, I'm down in the dumps.

Judy. But don't you want us to tell you some of the reasons why we feel so discouraged?

Therapist. If you did, you'd probably illustrate my point about how sharing negative thoughts can lower your sense of well-being.

Judy. Well, isn't it your job to listen to people's problems?

Therapist. Not really. My clients usually want me to help them find positive feelings and get closer to their mates.

Phil. Look, what I don't understand is this. You say if we feel negative, all we can do is talk negative, right? But then what? If we stop talking, we'll still feel upset and discouraged. So how can we change what we feel?

Therapist. Okay. Let's look at it this way. You've probably noticed your spirits go up and down during any given day. And as they go up and down, your view of the relationship changes, however slightly. When your spirits are up, the relationship looks better. Isn't that true?

Judy. I suppose so.

Therapist. Now, when we're in a low mood we're tempted to communicate, to let others know we're down. But if you can be a little patient, you'll see that those low moments will pass. When you go up just a little you'll notice you're entertaining more hopeful thoughts. Take the two of you sitting here right now. Each of you probably has hopes and dreams, and sees possibilities for the relationship. Maybe you don't want to trust those thoughts, but they're still there.

Judy. Of course they are or we wouldn't have bothered to come here.

Therapist. Each of you is probably seeing things a little bit differently than before, a little more optimistically. (They nod.) If you share these positive thoughts, they will help the relationship to spiral up. Believe me, these positive thoughts are just as real as the negative thoughts. It's only force of habit that makes you dismiss positive thoughts and stick with the negative.

Phil. I'd love to see us make a go of the marriage. I remember when we were first together; we were incredibly close, even though we had a really hard time making ends meet. Now we have a nice family and a good standard of living. We have every reason to be happy together. I miss being as close as we once were.

Therapist. See, those are the thoughts that raise the tone.

Judy. It hasn't been all your fault, Phil. I've been really irritable with you. I know I've been difficult. (Phil extends his hand and Judy grasps it.)

Judy. Do you think we can make it?

Therapist. Look at how close you feel right now and we have only just started talking. Those good feelings can be the dominant part of your relationship.

Phil. I just hope we can stay on this positive track.

Therapist. You have to learn to trust it. Any time you can share hopeful, high-spirited thoughts, your relationship will benefit. Positive thoughts are just as real as negative thoughts and feelings. In fact, they're more real! Negative thoughts are always associated with fears of the future and negative memories of the past, and only the present is real.

Judy. I feel better already. But what if we go back to our bad feelings after we leave here?

Therapist. You don't have to feel this way all the time to have a good marriage. You just have to remember that when you slip into the doldrums, your thoughts and perceptions will go with you. If that happens, don't take your thoughts too seriously. If you communicate those negative thoughts to each other, believe me, they'll seem more real. If you must share them, though, warn the other person it's your mood that's speaking, not you.

It's no coincidence that this chapter is the shortest one in the book. That's because communication isn't nearly as important as how we feel when we communicate.

Communication is to relationships what mopping up spills is to housecleaning. You need to clean up messes, but the idea is not to make them in the first place.

IN A NUTSHELL

- When your spirits are low is when you are most compelled to "talk about things" and least advised to do so. Many of the statements you make then will seem false or damaging from the perspective of a higher mood.

- If you must communicate when you are both down, head for the high ground—the positive and hopeful. You can always share possibilities and visions, discuss how difficult it is to see things accurately in a low mood, how much you want the same thing, how deceiving appearances can be and the things for which you're grateful. These subjects will lift your mood as you discuss them.

- Listen for the spirit behind the communication. When you are touched by feelings, you have gotten what that person has tried to say. You will feel enriched and the other person will feel heard.

- Use your level of closeness as a compass to assess how well your discussion is progressing. If, after ten minutes, you are feeling closer to each other, continue on the same track. If you feel more distant, stop, and give it another try later. If you want to continue, start all over and head the discussion in another direction. There is no such thing as progress in a discussion that alienates the participants.

4
MOODS
THE KEY TO UNDERSTANDING PEOPLE

"I know where it's at in life. The world we see in our low moods—struggle, suspicion, stress—is real life. The good times? They're just a break from reality that allows us to rest up before we reenter the fray."

The term "mood" is just a synonym for "feeling state." Almost all conflicts occur when the participants are in low moods. For some reason, people don't realize the connection between low moods and relationship dysfunctions. But once you know it, you know how to avoid the ravages of bad moods.

Here is how the process works. When our thinking is negative, our feelings and perceptions will exactly reflect those negative thoughts and feelings in that moment. If we trust those perceptions and feelings, our lives will take a turn for the worse. This chapter provides an in-depth understanding of how human feeling states (moods), if misunderstood, can interfere with well-being in relationships. The chapter reveals how we can have moods without moods having us.

THE MOOD MYTH

Isn't "getting to the bottom of it" the best way for a couple to handle a low mood?

THE GRAIN OF TRUTH

It's important for you to support your partner when he or she is feeling low.

THE CHANGE OF HEART

The best way to help a person in a low mood is to be understanding and overlook the effect mood has on his or her behavior. If you maintain your sense of well-being, your partner can make contact with your sense of well-being for support, much as a drowning person might reach toward someone on the shore. If you try to reach out and pull the person to shore, however, you are likely to end up in the water, too. Whatever mood a person is in is his present reality. If you try to coax him out of it, you are likely to end up in a low mood yourself.

There is no reason to "do anything" about a mood because our thinking is by nature transitory and our feeling state will always follow suit. Warmth, understanding, compassion and a respectful sense of humor are the only forces that can help a person who is struggling with a low mood.

There is no such thing as "getting to the bottom" of a mood. A person in a low mood thinks negatively. If you ask a man in a low mood why he's down, he will claim his thoughts are the cause. Someone in a high mood thinks hopeful thoughts.

WHAT MOODS ARE AND HOW THEY AFFECT PEOPLE

Mood, as defined by *Webster's Ninth New Collegiate Dictionary* (1989), means a "conscious state of mind or predominant emotion." When our mood is high, our spirits are up, and vice versa. Between the high and low points on the continuum are an infinite number of mood levels. Human beings constantly move up and down the mood continuum. Some mood shifts are dramatic and some are imperceptible.

As Mark Twain once said, "If you don't like New England weather, just wait a minute." Just as weather changes from day to day and even from hour to hour, so do our moods. Although meteorologists relate weather changes to alterations in atmospheric conditions, they cannot explain why atmospheric conditions change as they do. The same observation can be made about moods. No one really knows why our thinking suddenly changes the way it does, giving us a different feeling state. We may be sitting on a park bench pondering the beautiful possibilities of life. Moments later we are depressed and thinking about problems. What changed? Who knows? Change is the nature of moods, our "inner weather."

Although we may respond to our low moods differently, we all experience our low moods in similar ways. The thinking that creates low feeling states often has many of the following characteristics:

1. Our mental activity—or thinking velocity—increases.

2. Our thinking gravitates to problems and dissatisfactions.

3. We experience a heightened but distorted sense of immediacy. For example, we think we must do something right away about our circumstances.

4. We feel self-conscious. It seems we are the center of everybody's attention.

5. We have a pessimistic outlook. We notice limitations and are blind to possibilities.

6. We entertain many negative thoughts, emotions and concerns.

It is not the mood, the feeling state, itself, but how we relate to it that determines the quality of our life. It is our thoughts about our moods that cause us distress. We fear the moods are "real," that they will last forever. Understanding the relationship between thought and feeling determines our level of well-being independent of our moment to moment moods. *With this understanding we become grateful when our mood is high and graceful when it is low.*

Understanding how our thinking is related to our feelings and perceptions allows us to calibrate to moods. When people don't realize they have moods, they are hoodwinked into thinking it is "reality" that is changing, not just their thoughts. Their attempts to deal with "reality" then become like trying to catch a shadow.

If we look closely, we see our moods travel up and down a continuum, from high to low, all day long. We also notice our perceptions of life go along for the ride. Nothing in the world looks identical from one minute to the next.

All people tend to experience high moods in the same way—they're relaxed, energetic, in good humor, patient, carefree and compassionate. There is a large variation, however, in how people experience low moods. Some get aggressive and belligerent when they are down. Others become quiet and distant.

Moods, even low moods, provide an important function in the human experience. Moods are a navigational system. The specific feeling state we are in at a given moment tells us the quality of our thinking in that specific moment. We know that our thinking is the cause of the feeling even though we may not know what those specific thoughts are. Furthermore, the fact that an uncomfortable feeling state persists tells us that we have temporarily forgotten the thought/feeling connection. In other words, our feelings, when properly understood for what they are, provide the self-correcting mechanism in the human psyche. Just as physical pain informs us about what's happening in the body, emotional pain informs us about our thinking and understanding.

When people lose sight of the source of feelings, they mistakenly attribute their feelings to outside sources. They mistakenly think that our feelings inform us about the world at large. For example, we might think that our feeling of resentment about another person comes from what that person did to us. Dissatisfaction with our job means it's the wrong job for us. If we don't like a particular color we might think something is objectively wrong with that color. The basic question is this: are my feelings being generated from within via thought or are they being imposed on us somehow by circumstances and events beyond our control? The conclusion is that all feelings come from our thoughts. End of story.

ALTERED STATES

The drug culture says a person on drugs is in an "altered state of mind," which suggests a reality that's different from everyday reality. This book suggests that life is the experience of living in altered states of mind, all the time. Every time a mood shifts, it brings a new perspective, a different view of reality. What we see and think right now differs from what we saw and thought a few minutes ago. Life is a progression of altered states. There is no such thing as an unaltered state because we are always living in the experience of our thinking and our thinking is a moving target.

If life is an elevator, moods are the floors we visit. Let's explore five floors (among an infinite number):

1. *Gloom and Doom*
    My high school mates are doing so much better than I am.
    I'm getting old and my job is a dead end.
    Why is everyone always judging me?

2. *All Is Not Right With The World*
    There are many villains out there.
    I don't like my life.
    It's not fair that I put out fifty-two percent to my wife's forty-eight.
    I can see many defects in my job.

3. *I'm okay. Life's okay*
    My job is good when I have the right attitude.
    My mate isn't as bad as I thought.
    I feel contented.

4. *Gratitude*
    People are so well meaning.
    There are so many great jobs.
    I've got a better deal than my mate.
    Life is so interesting.

5. *Inspiration*
    My work energizes me.
    There is no way to go wrong in life.
    My mate is my best friend.
    I have more ideas than I can use.

SEEING PAST MOODS

Larry, 28, called to request marriage counseling. His wife, Helen, refused to be involved. The therapist suggested Larry come without his wife for at least the first session. The couple had been married for eleven years and had no children.

Larry. Our marriage has been very difficult and it's getting worse. I love my wife, but I can't go on like this much longer.

Therapist. What is the "this" you referred to?

Larry. Helen gets really angry. She gets verbally abusive and sometimes even physically abusive. She'll storm out of the house and not return for hours.

Therapist. How do you respond when she acts this way?

Larry. Sometimes I try to reason with her, but that seems to make things worse. To tell you the truth, I'm usually pretty disgusted when it happens. I defend myself as best as I can and wait for it to blow over.

Therapist. It sounds like you have a certain amount of perspective about it.

Larry. Not really. I'm really tired of it. I've run out of patience. It's particularly embarrassing to me when she flies off the handle in front of others. I don't see why she can't stop making such a fool of herself.

Therapist. What did your wife say about the prospect of counseling?

Larry. She wouldn't have any part of it. She won't even talk about it.

Therapist. I'm not surprised. She probably feels embarrassed about herself and feels she'll look like the "bad guy" in counseling.

Larry. We tried counseling two years ago and the counselor came down pretty hard on her. I must say, however, there was something to what the counselor said. I know that I have faults in the relationship but acting as out of control as she does is really unacceptable.

Therapist. Doesn't your heart go out to her when she's in such a troubled state of mind?

Larry. Why should it? I'm the one who's being mistreated and abused!

Therapist. You are both mistreated and you are both insecure. You suffer from her so-called abuse and she suffers from your harshness. If she weren't insecure, she wouldn't be angry. If you were more secure, you would be more compassionate.

Larry. Compassionate about what?

Therapist. When she goes into one of her tirades, doesn't she look troubled to you?

Larry. I never really noticed. I have all I can do to protect myself.

Therapist. Isn't it true Helen flies off the handle when she's in a low mood? When she isn't in a low mood, doesn't she display a more positive outlook on life and behave more appropriately?

Larry. Now that you mention it, much of the time she's a sensitive, happy person.

Therapist. Everyone spends the day in constantly shifting states of mind. When we're in a low mood, it's easy to feel insecure and to act out that insecurity in counterproductive ways. Helen's way of acting out her insecurity is to go into a tirade.

Larry. Wouldn't it be better for her to act it out in some other way? Why does she choose that way?

Therapist. People don't consciously choose how to act out their insecurity. They react habitually. A mood, a feeling state, is just a reflection of one's thoughts in a given moment. One of the qualities of a low mood is that it tempts us to act habitually, or the way we always act. We often do what our parents did when they were insecure. Helen's parents probably got mad and lashed out. This whole pattern of reacting to moods is all very innocent.

Larry. I don't get angry and act out when I'm in a bad mood.

Therapist. Do you see yourself as having moods?

Larry. Not really. Sometimes I might be disappointed or upset for a moment but then I'll just go on.

Therapist. Do you ever feel a little off-balance or not quite yourself?

Larry. No. Not at all. Well, sometimes I feel a kind of inner pressure. Is that what you mean?

Therapist. Is the tension or pressure an unpleasant feeling?

Larry. Definitely.

Therapist. Doesn't that pressure feel stronger sometimes?

Larry. Yes, sometimes I feel really pressured, and other times, not at all.

Therapist. That feeling of pressure is coming directly and exclusively from your thoughts in that moment. That is just the way we are wired up as human beings. We feel our thoughts. When your mood is high, there's no pressure. When it's low, you feel great pressure.

Larry. I see.

Therapist. How do you usually respond to that pressure?

Larry. I become more intense. I tighten my belt and work harder.

Therapist. And how does that work out for you?

Larry. Well, I've never really thought about it. Actually, I feel a little better, but I get worn out. Helen can always tell when I've had "one of those days." When I come home she always says, "You'd better sit down and relax, Larry. You look like you've been grinding away again."

Therapist. Helen probably doesn't understand why you get so intense about work.

Larry. No she doesn't. She asks me why I feel under pressure when I am so good and dependable at work. I wonder about that, too. Yet, I still feel it at times. It always seems like the work is pressuring me.

Therapist. Those thoughts of immediacy and importance that appear at those times are just thoughts but they don't look like thoughts. Once you recognize that fact, you won't be so compelled to wear yourself out. If you look, you'll see the outside world has not changed from five minutes ago, when you felt confident about the state of the world. It was only your thinking that changed. And your thinking created a feeling state of tension..

Larry. Helen doesn't seem to feel pressure the way I do.

Therapist. How do you know that?

Larry. She doesn't seem to get so knocked out.

Therapist. Her rampages are her way of acting out her bad moods. Everyone feels a different negative feeling in a low mood. When I'm down I feel rushed. Helen feels angry.

Larry. When I'm in a low mood I get intense.

Therapist. The specifics are determined by the particular thoughts that occur at those moments. What is the same is that the thinking changes. Helen, for example, might have scary thoughts about how threatening people are and how abused she is. She responds to those thoughts with angry feelings and she yells at you. In that mood, all those black thoughts seem like reality.

Larry. That sounds awful! What can I do to make things easier for her?

Therapist. If you could remember that thoughts and feelings coincide, you would be a comfort to Helen. You would also be less likely to get carried away by your work during your temporary moments of insecurity. Also, you wouldn't take Helen's words and actions personally when she's in a bad mood. You'd be able to relate to what she is going through. Your heart would go out to her—not in sympathy but in compassion for what it's like to be frightened by your own thoughts. As you begin to see past her moods, she will begin to see past them, too. Soon, moods will just come and go without any drama or conflict.

Larry. I do feel closer to her while we're talking like this. I've judged her and looked down on her because I didn't understand her. I'm a little embarrassed that I gave her such a rough time.

Therapist. We've all done what you've done.

IN A NUTSHELL

- Nothing needs to be "done" about moods. They come and go on their own. The less attention we give them, the better.

- When you are in a low mood, don't make important life decisions. Your thinking is not as sound as it is in a higher state of mind.

- When others are in a low state of mind, put everything they say or do in that context. Don't hold it against them or try to argue with them.
- Being understanding will help others to feel better.
- As you begin to see people's moods, you will see how to stay out of their way when they are low. You will also learn to what extent you can trust what they say and do.
- Stay open to the possibility that your mood might change at any minute. Just realizing that "it is just your thinking" will usher in new thought that will change your feeling state.

5
EMOTIONS MASTER OR SERVANT?

*"What a sucker she is.
She's so understanding she never feels bad."*

People generally handle emotion in one of two ways:

- They indulge their emotions and ride an uncomfortable roller coaster.
- They run away from them and become distracted and hardened.

There is a third alternative: *realize that emotions are only thoughts.* This chapter explains the true nature of emotions and how they function as subjectivity indicators. The view expressed in this chapter is a sharp departure from the current thinking of most therapists and marriage counselors. Yet clients who grasp the concept enjoy emotional stability, while staying in touch with their feelings.

THE NEGATIVE EMOTIONS MYTH

Don't negative emotions have to be expressed to clear the air?

THE GRAIN OF TRUTH

You want to be aware that you are in a negative frame of mind.

THE CHANGE OF HEART

Unpleasant or negative emotions are thoughts that contaminate the natural good feelings that exist between people. If you eliminate your negative thoughts, you will experience greater warmth and love toward your partner. Many current therapists recognize the importance of getting rid of negative thoughts and uncomfortable feelings in relationships. But how? Most therapists are under the mistaken impression that *expressing* these negative thoughts and emotions is the best way to eliminate them. Therapists call this *catharsis*, "the discharge of pent-up emotions" (*The Random House Dictionary*).

But even advocates of this theory admit catharsis will not permanently remove an emotion. At best, it will act as a "steam valve." The same emotion will return as soon as it is triggered by a new event or circumstance.

The only way to eliminate the harmful effects of negative emotions is through understanding. Once you understand what negative emotions are, and what they mean, your emotional states will have a positive effect on your life. Listed below are the realizations that can offset negative emotions:

- Negative emotions are just thoughts; they have no life of their own. When a thought is not in your mind, it does not exist.

- Negative emotions only rear their ugly heads when we are in a troubled state of mind. When we are feeling magnanimous, we experience positive thoughts.

- You will see that the same event or person provokes different feelings when your state of mind changes. You might see a car as a "clunker" if you're in a bad mood—and a "classic" in a good one. You might view the same person as "stingy" from a low state of mind and "thrifty" from a higher one.

It is possible to see anyone with understanding. There is always someone who appreciates the people we see in a negative light. For example, one man's shrew of an ex-wife is another man's dream come true. We all have the innate capacity to view that person as her admirers do. It is not in our genes to view her negatively.

The easiest way to rid your mind of negative emotions is to dismiss them as you would any distracting thought. If you were enjoying your eighty-dollar seats at the opera and began wondering whether to put new seat covers in your car, you would dismiss the thought. There's no way you'd let it interfere with your enjoyment of the opera. If you were enjoying being with your wife and suddenly remembered she forgot to put gas in the car, you might banish that thought to keep it from interfering with your evening at home.

We constantly can and do dismiss thoughts we deem extraneous and nonproductive. It is only our misguided judgment about what is extraneous and unproductive that supports the presence of negative thoughts in relationships.

Emotions serve one purpose in life: they are a mood indicator. The more unpleasant the emotions, the lower the mood. Negative emotions such as anger and regret are personal reactions to life. They arise when our level of understanding is low. The blacker the emotion, the more personally or subjectively we are reacting to life. Conversely, when we see life with perspective we experience pleasant, positive feelings. Our perceptions are more dispassionate. By using our emotions as a gauge, we can accurately assess how much to trust our perceptions at any given moment.

WHAT EMOTIONS ARE AND HOW THEY SERVE US

Emotions are born of thought. Sadness only exists in our lives when we think sad thoughts. When we realize that emotions are just more thoughts, they lose their power to distort our lives and distress us. Like other thoughts, they will pass. When we stop thinking them, they die.

Many current therapy approaches treat emotions as if they were tangible objects lodged in the mind. But emotions are no more real than dreams. No one fears that last night's dream has the power to affect our waking life. If we dreamed we ran out of gas on the highway, we would not walk to a gas station first thing in the morning. Emotions should be seen in the same light. They only have the power to affect us when we are actively thinking them.

Emotions are mirages of the mind. Are mirages real? Certainly. Mirages are real mirages. Any physicist knows the angle of the sun, your vision and the slope of the ground can converge and cause you to see water where none exists. Viewed from the senses, the mirage is real. Viewed from a higher, broader perspective, the mirage is illusory.

Human emotions are illusory in the same way. The following vignette illustrates this:

> The scene is the lobby of a movie theatre. You are standing in line to buy tickets. Suddenly a burly man walks in front of you and steps on your toe. He offers no apology. In fact he acts like you don't exist. Anger builds in you.

Suddenly, your anger turns to chagrin. You just noticed his white cane and black glasses. Turning to the man behind you, you relate your mistake. He laughs and says he knows this alleged blind man. "That man is not blind," he reports. "He's just a sadist who pretends to be blind to avoid punishment for his sadistic acts."

Your embarrassment instantly turns to outrage. "How could anyone be that low?" you ask yourself. You consider taking a punch at him despite his size.

An older man pulls you aside. He tells you that the man behind you is the sadist and the burly man actually is blind. Your outrage turns to confusion and then levity when a middle-aged, bald-headed man comes over and says, "Smile, you're on Candid Camera!"

In this example, each emotion was a mirage created by the convergence of circumstance, perception and interpretation. Each emotion was understandable in context. As the interpretation changed, the emotion changed accordingly.

Now imagine, you are engrossed in an intense discussion with a friend. You both feel upset and despondent. Suddenly, you are told there is a fire in the building. You rush to help put out the fire. Are you still upset? Of course not. You can't afford to be. You need all your attention to concentrate on putting out the fire.

In a way, your bad feelings were preempted by the fire. When the fire is doused, would the despair return? Probably not; you would be relieved and exhilarated. The earlier discussion might seem silly. What happened to the emotions that were once so real and important? They were just temporary indulgences to be tabled in the face of important matters.

If emotions can be set aside during emergencies, can they be set aside anytime? Sure. They are only illusions.

All too often, people treat emotions as if they offer information about life. If they feel anger toward someone, they believe that person did something to justify it. If they feel dissatisfied, they assume there must be something wrong with their lives.

Emotions are never a statement about the world around us. They are always a statement about our momentary perspective on life. Emotions are a quality-control device that measures the quality of our thinking. They tell us whether or not we are viewing life dispassionately—and how sound our judgment is. When we experience black emotions like anger and despair, we know that we are taking things too personally and have lost touch with the big picture. When our feelings are positive and light we know we are viewing life with more wisdom and perspective.

Suppose you are walking in the street and a person bumps into you. You could react to this minor incident in many different ways:

- If you take the incident very personally, you will say to yourself, "Why did that guy do that to me? Why does everyone treat me badly?" You feel resentment or anger.

- If you see the incident less personally, without any malice, you might think to yourself, "Why don't people pay more attention to where they are going?" You feel impatient.

- If you see the incident with more perspective, it might seem humorous to you. You might reflect on people's propensity to get in each other's way, innocently.

As you take the incident less personally, your feelings become more positive. Your emotions are always a perfect indicator of how subjectively you are viewing life. Emotions do not provide information about the world around us. They do serve as a compass that indicates the quality of our thinking and our present capacity to make sound judgments.

THE SOURCE OF EMOTIONS

Emotions are garden-variety thoughts that have gotten excellent press in the psychological community. Like other thoughts, emotions grow when you pay attention to them. Once upon a time a person got angry now and then—"No big thing. So what?" After anger got all that press, it was, "Wait a minute. I am angry. Something important is happening here," as if anger were some alien force with a life of its own. A goldfish will grow as the size of its pond permits. Emotions are like goldfish. They will grow to any size depending on how much attention they get.

    The emotions we grew up with seem like reality to us. If our parents were prone to anger, for example, we would accept that as "normal." We would hear people routinely say things like, "He's angry." "Why is she angry?" or "Does that make you angry?" We would assume that anger must be a big part of life, not just a part of a thought system. We would get used to feeling anger. Anger would be real for us.

    How do you know if a negative feeling has become real? It always has the following characteristics:

- It has an unpleasant feeling.
- You feel it often.
- It seems like circumstances create that feeling. If you feel rushed, for example, it seems the world was designed

with too few hours and too much to do. If you feel sad, the world seems full of sad occurrences.

As our sense of inner security goes up and down, we notice the onset of different types of feelings. The more insecure we are, the darker and more compelling the feelings. As our sense of well-being rises, our feelings are more light and pleasurable. Let's look at the range of thoughts associated with various feeling states:

BLACK THOUGHTS:

Feelings range from serious to grim. Self-conscious. Circular thinking. Pessimism. Emergencies. "Is this all I have to show for my efforts in life?"

GRAY THOUGHTS:

Stress, problems, resentments, dissatisfaction and boredom. Thoughts of judgment, comparison and fault-finding. Lots of likes/dislikes, good/bad, needs and wants. Inclination to disagree with others. "Life is so hard."

WHITE THOUGHTS:

Peace of mind. Lightheartedness and satisfaction. Easy to enjoy other people. Easy to relax. "Life is so interesting."

SILVER THOUGHTS:

Enjoyment and appreciation. Creativity and insight. Contagious happiness. People are endearing. "Life offers so many possibilities."

GOLDEN THOUGHTS:

Feelings of gratitude. Humor everywhere. Genius. Strong desire to contribute to others. "I'm in love with life."

Negative emotion tells us our mental health is suffering, just as physical pain signals that we are abusing our bodies. A change in perspective is needed to right our thinking and regain feelings of well-being.

THEY TALKED UNTIL IT HURT

Barbara and Randy, both in their late 20s, have been married for two years. They have no children. They feel they have a very healthy relationship. They came in for therapy because a problematic pattern in their relationship was getting worse.

Barbara. It's not that our marriage isn't working. Most of the time it's great. It is just that when we talk sometimes, we both end up feeling bad. I don't know what we're doing wrong.

Therapist. Randy, do you share your wife's perceptions?

Randy. Yes. We have a nice thing going. It's just that there are a few things that bother me.

Therapist. It sounds like you have a lot of appreciation for each other. That's the most important thing in a marriage.

Randy. Here's what happens. Once in a while, she'll do something that really galls me. I know it isn't a big deal, but I feel full of resentment. It builds until I tell her. If I can just express it, it will go away.

Barbara. And when he does express his resentment, wow! Is he ever intense. It frightens me. Then, often I think I did something wrong and I feel so guilty, I get defensive. Next thing you know, we're in a fight.

Randy. I don't know what else to do. In my last marriage, I didn't express my resentments and they built up. I don't know what to do.

Therapist. You two have more than enough goodwill and respect toward each other. All you need is a little understanding of how people function psychologically. You'll begin to see that resentments are just thoughts that can be dropped. Anyone can learn how to keep his or her head clear of resentments. All you have to do for now is to learn to drop thoughts. Ultimately the principles I teach will enable you to avoid resentful thoughts altogether.

Randy. That's what I am doing. My way of dropping thought is expressing my resentments to Barbara. You know, hashing them through, dealing with them and being done with them.

Therapist. Randy, would I lose credibility with you if I suggested that expressing your resentments is not the best way to deal with them?

Randy. I don't see any other way.

Therapist. Actually, all you're doing is following a ritual: you give yourself permission to drop the thought as soon as you express it. What you do is no different from the person with a lot of plans on his mind. As soon as he puts them on a "to do list," he gives himself permission to forget them. He certainly had the capacity to forget them earlier. He was just following a ritual that he didn't realize was a ritual.

Randy. But if I don't express my resentments, they keep building up.

Therapist. Resentments are just thoughts, Randy. When you stop thinking them, they disappear. If Barbara bounced a check, for example, you might hold the thought of that incident in your mind. You would also hold in your mind the unpleasant emotions that accompany the memory. Are you with me so far?

Randy. Yes. That's exactly how my mind would work if Barbara did something stupid like bounce a check.

Therapist. Negative thoughts that sit in our minds tend to take on increased focus and importance. They're like a burr under a saddle that causes more irritation the longer it stays there. This increased focus and importance cause what you referred to as the "build-up" in your head. But these thoughts don't have a life of their own. They gain importance and attention only because you give it to them.

Randy. Well, how do I drop them?

Therapist. You just drop the thought of resentment the same way you drop any other thought. If, during this therapy session, you started thinking about what you might have for dinner tonight, chances are you would drop that thought. You probably would consider it an unacceptable distraction from something more important.

Randy. I'd usually just drop any distracting thoughts. But we're not talking about any old thought here. We're talking about resentment.

Therapist. The importance you place on a thought is subjective. The importance you assign it determines the power that thought has over you. In this case, you've given great importance to resentments. You believe resentments are more important and less "dismissible" than other thoughts.

Randy. Are you suggesting that some people can drop thoughts of resentment just as easily as they can drop thoughts of dinner plans?

Therapist. Some people even have trouble dismissing thoughts about dinner.

Randy. Hmm—this is pretty startling. I always assumed resentments were a force to be reckoned with.

Barbara. But it explains a lot of things to me, Randy. I mean look, you know how easily I can dismiss resentments. I always forgive and forget within a few minutes, right? I never understood why you couldn't do that. But me, I'll grapple with guilty thoughts for days on end. I couldn't understand why guilt didn't haunt everyone.

Therapist. You see, each person's belief system writes the script and we innocently act it out.

Barbara. I don't understand what you said, but I do feel I can see the light at the end of the tunnel.

Randy. I still don't see myself just dropping resentments. I've never done that before.

Therapist. There's a first time for everything. Just consider the possibility, Randy. You'll begin to notice yourself actively holding onto certain thoughts. Once you see that happening, the whole issue of thought and reality will feel increasingly different to you. It's very common for clients to start thinking differently and carve out a new reality for themselves. Now, let's talk about seeing life in a way that doesn't generate resentments in the first place. It all boils down to how you think…

IN A NUTSHELL

- Don't take negative emotions seriously; they provide information about the state of your mind, not the state of the world.

- When your thinking is contaminated by negative emotions, make as few decisions and engage in as few interactions as possible. This keeps these emotions from spilling over into your life.

- When negative emotions occupy your mind, quiet your thinking until they pass.

6
COMPASSION OR RESENTMENT? THE CHOICE IS YOURS

"I don't want to be compassionate because they might think it's okay to make mistakes."

Many clients think being "wronged" causes resentment as surely as sun exposure leads to sunburn. Not so. If your heart goes out to the "wrong-doer," you will feel compassion rather than resentment. To carry the previous simile a step farther, compassion is like an internal "suntan oil" that leaves us with a warm feeling inside rather than a burn. It is natural, useful and appropriate to feel compassion when you see another's innocence and pain. But people don't understand compassion. They confuse it with sympathy and with being a doormat. This chapter debunks the idea that we have to become hardened and angry to cope with life. This chapter will give compassion the place in life it deserves: it is the internal lubricant that protects human beings from each others' frailties.

THE COMPASSION MYTH

Isn't there such a thing as being too understanding?

THE GRAIN OF TRUTH

There is such a thing as acting against your better judgment because you feel sorry for someone.

THE CHANGE OF HEART

Compassion is a wonderful, warm feeling. To suggest you could have too much of it is like suggesting you could have too much joy or too much health.

When people say, "I was too understanding," they usually mean they used bad judgment because they felt guilty or sorry for the person. They acted that way to relieve those unpleasant feelings. As you know, unpleasant feelings distort our thinking and lead us to actions we later regret.

When we feel compassion, we are in a healthy state of mind. We have the wisdom to know how to respond to the troubled person. We clearly see without the distortion of negative emotion. We don't regret our actions.

Compassion is misunderstood and undervalued. Without compassion and understanding, interpersonal friction erodes the good feelings in a relationship. Compassion is our innate interpersonal lubricant. It is a blanket of warm feelings that protects us from the rough edges of personalities. When our heart goes out to another person, these warm feelings automatically fill our minds and hearts. Were we not filled with compassion, we could be bothered by the other person's behavior.

Whenever people exhibit counterproductive behavior, you can be sure they are in an insecure state of mind. If they were feeling more secure, they would have the wisdom to avoid those behaviors. When we perceive counterproductive behaviors in others, our response is either resentment or compassion. We feel resentful if we focus on the behavior and how it affects us. We are compassionate if we look beyond the behavior to the troubled state of mind that motivated it. We remember how this state of mind wreaks havoc with our common sense. Our hearts go out to the person.

Compassion also protects us against harsh self-judgment. We gain tolerance of our own imperfections. When we feel compassion we can identify with the humanness of life's predicaments. We are reminded of how we all occasionally get lost in our thoughts and lose our perspective. Our feelings of humanity are rejuvenated and our spirits rise. The other person gains hope because our spirits have risen from contact with him or her.

Thus, compassion helps the troubled person as much as it protects you. Warm, respectful, hopeful feelings are the best gift you can give a person in distress. Compassion provides the proper emotional environment for the person to recover his or her sense of security. Compassion always delivers an "I understand" message.

COMPASSION OR RESENTMENT—THE FORK IN THE ROAD

When another person appears to be imposing on us, we are at a crossroads. One fork in the road takes us to resentment, and the other to compassion. Which road we take depends on whether we think of ourselves or the other person. The following illustrates one person's experience of the two forks in the road.

THIS ROAD LEADS TO BITTERNESS	THIS ROAD LEADS TO GRATITUDE
R	G
E	N
S	I
E	D
N	N
T	A
M	T
E	S
N	R
T	E
	D
	N
	U
an uncomfortable feeling from the head	a warm feeling from the heart
focus on how it affects YOU	focus on how it affects the OTHER person

Five-year old Erika woke up in the middle of the night with an earache, her first one ever. When her father came in, he knew she was in intense pain. She was holding her ear and screaming. He dressed her, wrapped her in a blanket and headed for the Emergency Room. She cried incessantly, writhing in her seat. The more she cried, the more his heart went out to her. "What pain she must be in," he thought. "She has been crying steadily for half an hour now."

They checked into Emergency and were told to take a seat. The nurse apologetically told him it would be at least a half hour wait. The room had that vacant look that comes with fluorescent lighting. The chairs were wooden, the furnishings stark. The ten people waiting looked tired and grim. There was no talking, no whispering.

By this time Erika's crying was down to a whine, as she struggled to fall asleep. She nodded off every now and then, only to wake up and cry. Her father's heart went out to her. Her whining got louder. Suddenly she awoke, crying, and grabbed his neck. He could tell the pain had increased. His compassion rose.

After twenty minutes, a tall man walked up to the father. "Why don't you take your kid out of here until your turn?" he said. "We are sick to death of hearing her cry and whine." The father was taken aback. Then he realized that the man did not feel compassion for Erika.

Compassion insulated the father from the annoyance of the crying sounds. The other man had no such protection. To him, all that existed was the noisy crying and its effect on his nervous system. He could not see beyond these physical sensations to Erika's pain.

Then the father realized he stood in the same shoes as the other man. The father felt no compassion for the man even though he was suffering enough pain to bring him to the hospital, pain exacerbated by Erika's wails. Because the men were blinded by their insecurities, each felt resentment rather than compassion.

Everyone in the waiting room was at the same crossroads. Those who responded to Erika's crying with compassion found they experienced more warm feelings as the decibel level rose. Those who took the road of resentment found their uncomfortable feelings increased as noise mounted.

Many people assume that resentment, although unpleasant, protects us from being hurt by other people; they reason that if we feel understanding or compassion, we will become door mats. In fact, there is nothing more impractical in life than resentment. Compassionate feelings protect us. Resentment and hate obstruct our view of life and impair our objectivity. When people's heads are filled with hate and resentment, they tend to stumble into the same situation that "caused" the resentment in the first place. Feelings of compassion, on the other hand, are a clear window for an objective view of life. Compassion protects us from reacting unproductively to the behavior of others. It calms us down and makes us feel more secure.

To feel resentment, you look for malice and notice how incidents affect you. To feel compassion you notice the pain that motivated negative behavior. A compassionate vantage point is similar to the experience of watching a movie. We see the characters for what they are. We see exactly what they are likely to do and not do. As we watch the movie, our vision is not distracted by judgments and evaluations. We have maximum attention on the movie and minimum focus on how the action affects us. We have wide-angle vision.

Our level of compassion has a definite effect on other people. People exhibit less frailty in the face of compassionate responses. Notice, for example, how people relax and perform better in the presence of a supportive person than they do under the watchful eye of a perfectionist. This explains why people who have a high level of compassion bring out the best in others.

COMPASSION VERSUS SYMPATHY

Human connectedness comes in two forms: sympathy and compassion. When we sympathize, we identify with another person's specific plight. We relate it to a similar event that happened to us and re-experience all the same emotions. When we are compassionate, however, we connect with the general human feeling of the other person. The following example illustrates the difference between these two forms of human contact.

Assume you are listening to a friend whose son just dropped out of high school. Sympathy requires that you recall a time when you experienced a similar hardship. This recollection is bound to bring back the painful feelings that accompanied that event. Now you are both troubled, and you feel distant from the speaker because your attention is on your memories, not on him. Were you to listen to the same story with compassion, you would identify with the general feelings of caring and concern the father feels for his son. You would realize how valuable such caring is. You would feel close to both father and son.

Sympathy is emotionally bankrupting. Even the bittersweet, pleasant experience of watching a soap opera is draining, unless you watch it with understanding. Certainly, we all want to feel a connection with others. We don't want to be turned off to others in their hour of adversity. These feelings of identity and understanding allow us to be appropriately patient with the frailties of others (and ourselves.) Sympathy and commiseration, however, are undesirable forms of human connectedness. Other forms of connectedness exist that work much better.

Many psychotherapists and counselors get caught in the trap of sympathy. If they identify with their client's problems, their own mental health suffers.

When therapists tire of "taking client problems home," they often jump from the frying pan into the fire by becoming emotionally hardened. They intentionally turn off their feelings of sympathy to insulate themselves from patients' stress. Patients experience these therapists as distant and aloof. The therapists, in turn, become alienated and bored.

True compassion is the savior of psychotherapists' job satisfaction, enabling them to stay in touch with clients' human side without suffering emotional pain. Clients experience "being understood" and therapists benefit from the warm, human connection.

To find compassion, one must look beyond specific problems to the basic human elements involved. If a person is sad because her mother died, the listener must look beyond the death to the basic human experience of disappointment. If a person is angry, the listener must look beyond the situation to the pain we feel when we lose sight of another's innocence.

Compassion reminds us of our own humanity. It lets us relate to others without getting involved in the details. When we feel compassion for others, their spirits will rise because we appreciate their distress, yet our spirits remain high.

The essential point to remember here is that sympathy forces us to re-experience painful memories. Compassion, on the other hand, is a here-and-now recognition of the true nature of life—that we all get crunched by our thought systems sometimes. Therapists who have discovered compassion claim their jobs keep them humble, vital and warmly connected with their fellow human beings.

The chart below summarizes the differences between these two types of human connectedness:

	SYMPATHY	COMPASSION
Accompanying Feeling:	Sadness	Warmth
What You Identify With:	The Specific Problem	The Impersonal Fact of Pain and Loss in Life
How You Feel Afterwards:	Drained	Exhilarated
How They Feel Afterwards:	Concerned	Expanded and Strengthened

THE COMPASSION CONTINUUM

The shopkeeper yells at customer 'A' and customer 'B'. 'A' gets angry. 'B's heart goes out to the shopkeeper. Why the two different reactions to the same incident? Is it in their genes to react as they did? No. Did they hear different words coming from the shopkeeper's mouth? Probably not. 'A' and 'B' entertained a different set of thoughts during the incident. These thoughts left them feeling differently. 'A' thought about the insult of being talked to in that way. These thoughts led to feelings of resentment. 'B' thought about the plight of the shopkeeper. These thoughts engendered feelings of compassion.

Compassion and resentment are different interpretations of life. Compassionate people and resentful people will defend and swear by their interpretation. A wise observer can see both interpretations. Once you can see both interpretations you can choose the life view you want.

Between the extremes of compassion and anger/resentment, there exists a wide range of responses to a given situation. Let's explore this continuum.

TAKING IT PERSONALLY

"Why does he think he can get away with treating me that way? Do I look like a wimp?" You read malice into the situation. You feel outraged and vengeful.

UPSET

"He shouldn't treat me that way." Behavior is seen as intentional. You feel angry and upset.

BOTHERED

"That guy shouldn't lose his cool like that." Behavior is seen as negligent and unacceptable. You feel irritated and annoyed.

ACCEPTING

"It's interesting that a person who deals with the public would lose his cool so easily." Behavior looks innocent. You find the incident interesting.

UNDERSTANDING

"That fellow must have had an awfully hard day to be provoked so easily." You see the insecurity behind the behavior. Your heart goes out to him. You feel warmth, compassion.

AMUSED

"We all have our moments." You see the big picture and enjoy it.

IN A NUTSHELL

- Remember that compassion helps you *and* others.
- Believe that every person deserves to be understood. There is probably someone who would list you as an exception to this rule just as you may be tempted to list others.
- To find compassion, look beyond the behavior to the troubled state of mind that motivated the behavior.

7
DISSATISFACTION
A MENTAL ILLNESS

"I've got class. I am such a discriminating person that no one is good enough for me. My sister has zero class. She is indiscriminately happy."

People assume that expressing dissatisfaction is the first step toward satisfaction, but experience shows it is more often the first step toward creating hard feelings. An overwhelming percentage of "this-bothers-me-will-you-please-change" dialogues end up unhappily—with arguments, resentments, self-consciousness and guilt. Why? People tend to be sensitive about their so-called frailties. This sensitivity grows when somebody in a low mood points them out.

Dissatisfaction does to relationships what rust does to cars. A focus on dissatisfactions creates a negative tone that undermines and weakens a relationship. That negative tone makes it less likely that the other person will see and correct his/her mistakes.

You don't have to take my word for this. Read this chapter and see if the logic is compelling.

THE DISSATISFACTION MYTH

Won't resentments build in a relationship unless annoying behaviors and dissatisfactions are brought up?

THE GRAIN OF TRUTH

A relationship does need a self-correction mechanism.

THE CHANGE OF HEART

"Okay, close your eyes so you can't see everyone else's answers." The hundred people in the room shut their eyes. "Select a relationship in your life– it can be your marriage, your relationship with your children or your relationship with your parents. In that relationship, has your heart been in the right place? Deep down, have you tried your best to do right by that person? If you feel you have done your best to be a good mate, parent, child or whatever, raise your hand." Every hand rises. "Now look at the other person in the relationship. Would you say deep down they had your best interests at heart? If you feel they have done their best to be a good mate, parent, child or whatever, raise your hand." About one-third of the hands go up.

This vignette speaks to the trust paradox: people easily see their own good intentions but have difficulty seeing the good intentions of others. In order for a relationship to work, an attitude of trust must be present. Mistrust leads to hurt feelings, manipulation and conflict. You achieve trust by realizing that, like yourself, other people mean well. At the least, you can adopt a benefit-of-the-doubt stance, giving people maximum opportunity to show their good intentions.

We all must live as if our partners have our interests at heart. If people didn't have those generous intentions, relationships would not be in the cards for humanity.

When the emotional atmosphere of the relationship is cold and negative, the participants back into a protective shell of ego. They begin to look out for themselves. The deeper they retreat, the less motivated they are to look out for the other person.

When a couple is relaxed and happy together they naturally look out for each other's interests. The goodwill they feel motivates them to please each other, and their relaxed state of mind enables them to see themselves objectively and implement self-correction. Common sense tells you when your behavior is out of line. The more secure a person feels, the greater his or her powers of observation. A person that tends to talk too loudly, for example, will notice that fact when he is sufficiently tranquil. Suddenly he will say, "Why do I talk so loud? I must think all people are deaf."

MIND-SETS—HOW THEY MAKE ILLUSIONS LOOK REAL

A mind-set is a rigid, limited way of seeing life, an automatic predisposition. A mind-set is like a pair of sunglasses: it colors the way life looks to you. For example, when people have a suspicious mind-set, they see suspicion everywhere. Perfectionists see imperfections wherever they look.

People often see their mind-sets as realities. Mind-sets share three important characteristics that make them difficult to recognize.

- They are self-validating. For example, suspicious people look for signs of betrayal and find it everywhere. They unwittingly interpret innocent actions as deceitful and detect deceitful actions where none exist.

- They are externally validating. Have you ever had a perfectionist looking over your shoulder? Perfectionists tend to make you nervous. You make more mistakes than usual. Perfectionists note these mistakes, of course, and the cycle continues.

- They lock you into an uncomfortable, but familiar, feeling state. A suspicious person lives in feelings of mistrust. A perfectionist lives in feelings of irritation. These feeling states are so familiar it is hard to imagine any other experience. Fortunately, all mind-sets provide an uncomfortable, unpleasant feeling. If we mistrust that feeling, we expose the mind-set for what it is.

"Medical school disease" illustrates what a mind-set is and how it affects you. Medical students often report having symptoms of the diseases they are studying. When all they think about is the disease, they have developed a disease mind-set. A more common example is the fear mind-set one might have when walking alone at night. Once a person has a predisposition for fear, danger lurks everywhere. A falling leaf, a shutter swinging or a person sitting on a porch might be interpreted as dangerous. This fear mind-set takes over no matter how safe the neighborhood. Freedom from this mind-set occurs when the person realizes his or her thinking is what is so scary and dangerous.

Anything we spend a lot of time thinking about will become a mind-set. People who tend to think about food, for example, find thoughts of food consuming their consciousness. A mind-set is a habit we adopt out of insecurity. A critical and dissatisfied mind-set feeds on itself, determining what we think and see and how we react.

In a dissatisfaction mind-set, our eyes are always seeking—and finding—dissatisfaction. The world or our partner are just not up to snuff.

HOW DISSATISFACTION AFFECTED AN ORGANIZATION

John owned a small real estate firm. One weekend, he attended a seminar on interpersonal communication. The seminar leader said dissatisfaction builds up in people if it is not expressed. He recommended that participants sit down with others and allow them to get repressed dissatisfaction "off their chests." He called these meetings "withhold sessions," or opportunities to express feelings that were being withheld.

The next Monday, John called a "withhold meeting" for fifteen employees. He asked them to express any dissatisfaction on their minds. The employees were surprised by his request. There was a five-minute silence before Rita, the bookkeeper, spoke up. "I don't like it when everything is put on my desk at the last minute with a note that says *Rush*." John thanked Rita for getting the ball rolling and waited for others to speak. Three other people spoke up—they had no serious concerns. People liked working there. The meeting lasted twenty minutes. Everyone agreed the meetings should become a regular event.

By the tenth withhold meeting, John was totally disillusioned. It was taking up more and more time. The second meeting had taken twenty-five minutes; the next forty minutes. The third meeting took an hour and twenty minutes and ended prematurely. There was more than enough dissatisfaction each week to fill the time. "Where did all these problems come from?" he wondered. It also bothered John that the emotional tone of the meetings dropped from week to week. People were taking their dissatisfaction more seriously. In the first and second meetings, people expressed their problems in an off-hand manner. In the last meeting, people voiced dissatisfactions as if they were ground from the gut.

John had discovered the dynamic of dissatisfaction mind-set. Dissatisfaction had never been a big part of his employees' reality before he began offering withhold sessions. Of course, his employees had had occasional gripes but had dismissed them because they liked their jobs and wanted to get on with their work. When John introduced the idea of dissatisfaction to the group, his employees began to look for trouble. As time went on, they thought more and more about dissatisfactions and less and less about their work. Now they shared a dissatisfaction mind-set.

When John realized what had happened, he shared his thoughts at the next meeting. His employees laughed at what they had done. One of them said his wife had noticed how negative he had become. He responded by griping about her candor. The office howled. Everyone was glad to wake up from the nightmare.

THE HAPPY EXPERIMENT

Greg and Lori have been married for three difficult years of fighting, arguments and break-ups. Then they went to a seminar on relationships. The teacher talked on and on about being positive and staying away from negative thinking. He said expressing negative sentiments erodes goodwill. His ideas were revolutionary to Greg and Lori, who had been involved in confrontational encounter groups. They concluded the notion was well-meaning but unrealistic.

They did notice, however, that they had enjoyed the workshop. In fact, they felt closer than they had for some time. They were intrigued by how much the workshop had affected them.

As they lay in bed reading after the seminar, Lori had an idea: "Greg, what if we tried to be positive and nice to each other? We could experiment for one day and see what happened."

"One day?" Greg replied. "I don't know about that. It sounds a little contrived." Then Greg thought how nice it was when Lori was sweet. "Let's do it," he said.

They set up the experiment. They agreed that they could think whatever they wanted but could not say anything with a negative sentiment behind it. If one of them violated that rule, he or she had to give the other a twenty-minute massage. They realized how tortuous it would be to massage someone you're mad at. Twenty minutes would feel like six hours. The experiment would start when they woke up and would end at midnight.

The next morning it took about ten minutes for Greg to resent Lori. She woke him up early after he told her he wanted to sleep in. He kept still, but was grimly determined to mention it the next morning when the experiment was over. By noon, they had countless resentments on their minds. Greg regretted doing the experiment on a Sunday. On a weekday, they wouldn't have had as many hours together. Lori contemplated airing her list of accumulated resentments at 12:01 A.M.

As the day wore on, each found it easier to endure resentments. They were surprised at how often they were annoyed at each other and how petty most of the annoyances were. Because they did not immediately express their resentment, there was a "cooling-off" period, and the problems seemed to lose their punch.

When they awoke the next morning, they reflected on the previous day's experiment. To their surprise, they agreed it was the nicest day they had had together in recent memory—more laughter, more intimacy, more relaxation. They noticed they felt safe around each other knowing they wouldn't be attacked. Another surprise: they got over their dissatisfaction sooner than they ever would have imagined possible. Greg, for example, said he resented her leaving the car without gas, and thought it would bother him for a couple of hours. He forgot about it within ten or fifteen minutes.

Greg and Lori had no resentments to share. Every gripe of the previous day had disappeared from their minds and, when they looked back, gripes seemed silly. Before the experiment, they thought dissatisfaction was important and needed to be expressed. Their minds operated like a revolving door: the resentments came and went.

Would they repeat that experiment? No. It was too much work to fight the habits of being negative. What they did was more radical. They adopted a positive direction in their relationship as a way of life. The experiment proved that living in positive feelings was available. They each set a course in the right direction without trying to force it. With time, their relationship became more positive. They simply did not think of dissatisfactions very often. It wasn't long before they didn't even have to work at being positive. They had changed their mentality.

HOW TO BE CRITICAL WITHOUT BEING DISSATISFIED

There are many professional critics who are paid to help people decide how to invest their entertainment dollars. Every critic has a private life and her husband and kids may not all be that grateful for her discerning critical eye. The critic must learn not to take the job too seriously. Criticism is a game to be played. Just as a football player knows that he can't use a crossbody block to get to the dinner table faster, a critic knows her work tactics are appropriate to the office, not home.

Actors walk a fine line between game-playing and real life. An actor portraying a depressed person must leave that negative outlook at the theatre or he'll ruin his life.

Critical faculties are sometimes useful in life. If your mate asks you which outfit to buy, it would not be appropriate to say, "Don't ask me, I don't want to get into being critical." Just remember: if you don't take your dissatisfaction and criticism too seriously, you will never develop a critical-dissatisfied outlook.

DISSATISFACTION—THE THOUGHT PROCESS

It is commonly understood that worry causes upset stomach and occasionally ulcers. The worrier has a tight stomach because he is actively creating fearful thoughts. Taking away today's concerns doesn't leave the habitual worrier carefree; he'll just come up with a new list. The sour feelings suffered by the dissatisfied are similarly self-inflicted. Today's complaints and criticisms are merely the most recent "cause" of dissatisfaction. The dissatisfied person is predisposed to seeing faults and shortcomings in the same way that the worrier is predisposed to see what might go wrong. Dissatisfaction is a thought process that brings unhappiness. The alternative to worry and dissatisfaction is enjoyment. We can use the mind to enjoy life or we can use it to judge, analyze and compare what we see.

Let's put Appreciation at one end of a yardstick and Annoyance at the other. The "it" on the yardstick below could be anything—a person, an event or an object.

The experience:	The life that the experience leads to:
Galled by it	Ulcers and nervous disorders
Bothered by it	An emotional roller-coaster
Irritated by it	A stressful existence
Interested in it	A lighthearted, interesting life
Appreciating it	A high-toned, contented life
Enjoying it	A contagious happiness
Thrilled about it	An exuberant, inspired life

Where you are on this yardstick at any given moment determines your level of happiness, satisfaction, stress and rapport with others. The yardstick exists within your head, not out in the world somewhere. Being bothered is a learned, habitual behavior that can be dropped once it is seen as nothing more than a thought pattern.

IN A NUTSHELL

- Remember, despite appearances to the contrary, your partner wants to be a good mate or friend just as much as you do.
- Problems in your relationship signal that warmth and affinity are low. Realize that you have probably fallen into a lower state of mind where your sense of perspective is severely compromised.
- Know that appreciation and trust are possibilities just as real as problems.
- Benign neglect—intentionally overlooking a thought—will often have positive effects on a relationship. Once you drop your ill will, your mate will feel more secure and will be likely to correct the conditions that concern you. Benign neglect can free your mate from the pressure your dissatisfaction places on his or her ego.
- If you feel compelled to comment on another person's behavior, wait until you have a positive attitude and feelings of warmth and respect toward that person.
- Remember that discretion is the better part of valor. Unless there is at least a ninety percent chance that your talking to the person will improve matters, don't try it. If your action is unlikely to help, it makes little sense to add more ill will to the relationship.
- Approach the person as gently as possible to minimize the likelihood of defensiveness.

8
EFFORTLESS, PERMANENT CHANGE POSSIBILITY OR PIPE DREAM?

"I don't mind things changing as long as they don't end up different."

People don't believe they can change. They can see working at it, and maybe even changing a little for now, but permanent, effortless, substantial change looks like an impossible dream. I know different. People can change effortlessly, permanently, in an instant. I see it happen every day in my practice. Skeptics say, "How could major change happen suddenly? It has to take time." If you look at it logically, though, you realize that it has to happen suddenly. When you change, there is a single moment when everything is different.

The change process described in this chapter could properly be called "changing from the inside out." The only way we can really change is to change the way we feel inside. Our thinking changes our outlook, and our behavior follows suit.

THE CHANGE MYTH

Isn't it true that people can't change?

THE GRAIN OF TRUTH

People find it difficult to change their behavior patterns at will.

THE CHANGE OF HEART

Everyone has the capacity to change, and it helps to understand how it occurs. People change by becoming more themselves and less their conditioning. When a person gets insecure, he retreats to his conditioned personality, a coat of armor made of bad habits and pretenses. In our personality armor, we're clumsy, inappropriate and unresponsive—we don't deal well with life. We don the armor because it's familiar and offers safety when we feel insecure. When we feel secure again, we put the armor aside. Our behavior is now guided by common sense. Everyone is delightful and productive when operating without armor.

The way to facilitate change is to treat people with understanding and goodwill. Goodwill quells insecurity. It invites people to drop their armor and be themselves. When the armor goes, people regain the innate assets of wisdom, creativity, humor and compassion—assets that increase productivity and responsiveness in life. Without armor, these positive human qualities will flower.

When Jim gets insecure at work he puts on an armor called "frenetic." By the time he gets home to Elaine he is wound up like a spring. She reacts to this tension by becoming irritable, forcing him deeper into his shell of tension.

When Elaine sees that insecurity is causing Jim's freneticism, she becomes compassionate and warm toward him. He relaxes and the tension starts to dissipate. Soon, the contrast between his relaxed feeling at home and his overwrought feeling at work helps him get his perspective. Gradually, he learns to keep his bearings under pressure.

A human being can be likened to a flower. In a climate of emotional well-being, a person grows toward his or her potential. Understanding and goodwill are the food and water that nourish the blossom.

HOW PEOPLE CHANGE

People tend to go through predictable stages in dropping a conditioned habit. (Not everyone goes through every stage, and the time spent in each stage varies.) The following outline will help you understand the stages of personal change:

OBLIVIOUS

John has always been verbally abusive. He yells at people at the drop of a hat. When you ask him why he is abusive he yells, "I'm not abusive." He means what he says. In his mind he is not abusive. A person in the oblivious stage needs to have an experience that represents a vivid contrast to what is "normal" in his world. John lives in a violent world. Most everyone reacts to him in kind, by fighting back. It will take a gentle, soft experience to touch him and set the change in motion.

I once had a client who was sarcastic. People hated being around him. I asked him if he knew he was hurting his employees' feelings. He was shocked at the suggestion. In his sarcastic way he told me he never hurt anyone's feelings. I asked if his own feelings ever got hurt. He looked puzzled by the question and then muttered, "No." It appeared to me, though, that my question itself hurt his feelings. I asked him and he denied it angrily. I knew he was telling the truth, by his reckoning. In fact, his feelings were hurt so often he didn't know what a safe, relaxed feeling was. Another contrast was in order here.

JUSTIFYING

Let's say someone resisted the temptation to be defensive and continued to be nice to John. He finally calmed down and felt soft and relaxed for the first time in weeks. Against the backdrop of this gentle feeling, his next abusive thought finally registers as abuse. John now sees he was often abusive. But because others usually reacted defensively and returned the abuse, John concludes his behavior was justified. What John needs now is to see a new way to respond to life, even in the face of someone else's abusive behavior.

This kind of insight usually comes during a lull between perception and behavior. If someone yells at John and he yells back instantly, he won't give his insight a chance to appear. If there is even a one-second lull before his response, however, he has a chance to get an eyeful. He sees that the other person is reacting from an insecure state of mind. If he sees this insecurity, his heart goes out to that person, and he sees the mutual abuse in a different light. He reads more innocence into it and less malice. John sees that barking back is an inappropriate and even silly way to respond to a frightened person. He now has a more complete understanding of his own behavior and his interactions with others.

COMPULSIVE AWARENESS

In John's view, his abusive behavior has gone from not existing at all (oblivious) to being a good strategy (justified) to being a bad habit. John is now aware how often he thinks, talks and acts abusively—constantly, he thinks. His friends assure him he's less abusive than before—his new understanding has already changed him to some extent. But to him, his abusiveness is painfully clear. Now, it is only a matter of time before John drops his abusiveness entirely. How much time it takes depends on how much his thinking gets in the way. In the compulsive awareness stage, you should pay as little attention as possible to what you see. Seeing what you are doing in life is good. It prompts you to change. But reacting emotionally to what you see is not helpful. Any feelings of guilt, any willful attempts to change or analyze your behavior are misguided. It's sufficient for you to see you have counter-productive habits that disappear when you notice them.

CHANGE

John continues to live his life. One day he is returning a gift, but the clerk refuses to take back the toaster without a receipt. John hauls off and gives the clerk a tongue-lashing. Suddenly, John feels terrible—as if he ate some bad fish at lunch. He is not in shape to be abusive anymore. Now, being abusive registers on his sensitivities. He realizes with delight that it has been weeks since he raised his voice to anyone. He changed and he didn't even realize it. That is the way change ultimately occurs. It is so subtle you hardly notice it.

QUESTIONS AND ANSWERS ABOUT CHANGE IN A RELATIONSHIP

How do you change your partner?

With considerable difficulty, if at all. In case you haven't noticed, people resist others "working on" them. To help your partner change, you need permission—freely given without pressure or threat. With permission you become a team working under the "changee's" direction. For example, Tom admits he is overweight. Yet, when Sue, also concerned about his health, suggests he skip a dessert, he barks, "Mind your own business." Sue must have a heart-to-heart talk with Tom. When Tom sees Sue's goodwill he might say, "You could help me by asking if I really want dessert." Then Sue's comments no longer seem like nagging, but an expression of her caring.

My partner says he wants to stop smoking, yet he stubbornly resists my help. Where have I gone wrong?

Permission is not perpetual. I am a therapist and I frequently run out of permission from my clients. If I don't have enough permission the client becomes resistant, defensive. If your mate becomes stubborn, you have to reapply for permission. You need to get a new meeting of the minds.

Do you recommend mates helping each other to change?

Few couples get away with helping each other to change. Here's why: to help mates to change, you must totally accept them, as they are. Otherwise, they will resist your judgmental attitude. The inevitable result is an interesting paradox: those who have accepted their mates have low motivation to change them and those who haven't don't have the right attitude to do so.

HOW A JUVENILE DELINQUENT CHANGED HIS WAYS

If there was ever a person who looked terminally incorrigible, it was Dan. Sixteen-year-old Dan was mandated for counseling by juvenile hall. If Dan was bored on a Saturday night, he would take the bus to the end of the line, beat up the bus driver and walk home. It was hard to see an ounce of humanity in the way he lived his life. The only emotion he showed was disgust with having to go to juvenile hall because of his conduct.

8 ♦ Effortless, Permanent Change Possibility or Pipe dream?

When Dan sat across from me in the first session, I couldn't look at his face. His eyes were so menacing I experienced a twinge of fear when I made contact, so I intentionally looked anywhere but at his face. For the first few sessions Dan said not a word. He would come in, sit and glower for an hour. At the end of the hour he would get up and go, as if he were leaving an empty room.

So concerned I was about his lack of response that I called juvenile hall. I told them I felt bad about wasting his parents' money. They assured me counseling was mandated and Dan's parents understood. They also said that most mandated juvenile hall kids got nothing out of counseling. Their point was I should not take it personally.

During these sessions I talked to Dan in the same way I would any client. I told him he had feelings of happiness and goodwill inside him, feelings that make life worthwhile. I told him thoughts of insecurity preempt these positive feelings. I said that people do counterproductive things only when they lose their sense of well-being. These negative behaviors make sense in context because they offer temporary relief from the bad feelings. One person might seek relief through alcohol, while another might work compulsively. I suggested to him that there is no way—and no need—to run from these feelings. The feelings are just thoughts. When we are insecure or frightened, we all tend to act counterproductively. Once our thinking calms down, the good feelings return.

Because Dan did not do any talking, I had the time to express these hopeful ideas in many different ways. I gave examples from real life and cited movies. I wanted him to see he could change his feelings. I wanted him to realize his own thinking was the source of his ill will and the source of his future happiness.

I tried to remain as hopeful and positive as I could with Dan. I knew my goodwill was the most important thing I could give him. I knew everyone, including Dan, had feelings of happiness and the wisdom to lead a productive life. I just didn't know when, if ever, that wisdom would be touched in Dan.

In the sixth visit, there was a major breakthrough. At the end of the session Dan nodded to me as if to say, "Thanks!" To me it was as if he had come over and kissed me. That little nod was a dramatic jump in responsiveness. I couldn't wait to see what happened in the next session.

From then on, Dan remained silent but became more attentive. Finally, he broke the silence in the twelfth session and cried uncontrollably. He said I was wasting my time trying to help him. "You have no idea what I have done in my life. Deep down I am an evil person. I always have been. I am hopeless."

I knew Dan was feeling his humanity. He had been touched. I was exhilarated. "Maybe you looked hopeless before," I told him, "but you certainly don't now! The feelings you are having now are the feelings that lead to change."

"I'll never change! You are a Pollyanna."

"You've already changed. You used to think only of yourself. Now you are concerned about wasting my time. You are actually displaying a conscience."

"Well, you've tried to help me. You're a nice person," he said with softness in his voice.

"Could you beat someone up right now?"

"I couldn't hurt a flea right now. I feel grateful my mom got help for me. But I'm afraid that after I leave this room, I might go back to my old ways."

"Let's see what happens. At least you know you have it in you to be happy and to feel warm toward others."

Dan left the office with a smile on his face. His mother was shocked at the change in him and came in for reassurance. I told her when people change, it is sudden. Often they can barely relate to how they used to be. She asked if I thought the change was permanent. I told her some of it would be permanent; it remained to be seen just how much.

I knew from experience that once a person has a moment of truth, he or she is never the same. The realizations that occur in those moments shift one's perspective irrevocably. Although the good feelings might fade temporarily, the person will forever gravitate toward them.

Dan was full of questions and interest during our later sessions. He wanted to know about socializing, what to say to people in normal conversations. He was interested in all the things that had been irrelevant to him during his criminal stage. His immediate goal was to get a job. He wanted to know what one did in a job. His previous life was so skewed; he was a babe in the woods about everyday matters. I was pleased he wanted to lead a normal life.

Juvenile hall recognized the change in Dan. They told the court about his progress. He was sent back to his family. He guided his fifteen-year-old brother out of a life of crime. By age eighteen, Dan was an assistant manager in a department store. He looks at his early years of crime as one would look at a bad dream—with bewilderment and relief.

As I look back at Dan's case, I see it as evidence of the indomitability of the human spirit. All I really offered Dan was consistent goodwill and hope. People so want to live productive lives that goodwill and hope are often all it takes.

THE DOMINO EFFECT

Change is a domino effect: a thought generates a feeling that, in turn, motivates a behavior. For example, thoughts about smoking lead to the desire to smoke, which leads to smoking. Thoughts of anger lead to angry feelings and then to acting out anger. Thoughts about a loved one lead to a warm feeling and a kiss on the cheek.

If you want to change, trying to stop the last domino (the behavior) won't do the trick. The feeling is the first domino. It pressures you to behave in a certain way. Thus, if you try not to smoke when you still feel like smoking, you pit your willpower against your escalating desire. Similarly, if you feel angry and inhibit your expression of that anger, it will intensify.

Clearly, the way to change a behavior is to change the feeling that motivates the behavior—the first domino. You do this by changing your thoughts for example, if you have a *change of heart* about smoking, your thoughts about smoking will change. You will think about the hassles and liabilities of smoking, which will give you unpleasant feelings about smoking. These feelings will inhibit your desire to smoke. Anger patterns may be broken in the same way. First you learn to see life with more understanding. When thoughts of understanding replace angry ones, your feelings will motivate benign behaviors to replace aggression.

Habits are more compelling at some times than at others. As our level of well-being goes up we are increasingly insulated from the temptation of habits. Conversely, when we are insecure, habits seem to have a strong hold on us. Below is a scale linking our level of well-being to our ability to resist habits:

OBSESSED

In a very low mood. We lunge into habitual behaviors without seeing the thoughts that precede them.

COMPELLED

In a low mood. The thought of the habit is constantly on our minds. It seems irresistible to us. Our willpower has an uphill battle.

AT CHOICE

In a higher mood. The two thoughts—"to do" or "not to do"—carry equal weight. Willpower works at this level.

TEMPTED

In a high mood. The thought of the habit comes to mind occasionally. We can easily dismiss it knowing it is just a thought with no life of its own.

FREEDOM

In a very high mood. The idea of the habit doesn't even occur to us. This is the level where effortless change occurs.

The best way to change a habit is to raise your level of well-being—become happier. When you are happier, all your habits are easier to resist. If you raise your level of security enough, the habits won't even occur to you.

It is a mistake to struggle with your habits. In doing so you are likely to wear yourself out, become discouraged and end up making yourself insecure. The insecurity then fuels the habits to stay on the diet. This anxiety fuels the desire to eat. If the overweight person finds a good feeling, he or she finds this happy state of mind provides the wisdom to eat sensibly.

Psychologist Fritz Perls once said fear is misunderstood excitement. When we contemplate change, we get a bubble of energy. If we are in a state of well-being, we will feel exhilarated by that energy. If we are insecure, we will get frightened. Thus, our reaction to change is another clue to our state of mind.

IN A NUTSHELL

- With real change, we don't make it happen. Instead, we notice it after it has happened. This change happens because it doesn't occur to us to act in the old way.
- The internal factors—what we think, how we feel—are forces behind change. If you try to change at the level of behavior, you are trying to make the tail wag the dog.

9
BRINGING OUT THE BEST IN PEOPLE

"I don't understand it. The more pressure and humiliation I apply, the worse he responds. Could it be that people want to be treated with goodwill and respect? Nah."

Peter is a perfectionist. He looks over people's shoulders to judge their performance. It comes as no surprise that everyone is nervous around Peter and, therefore, more prone to make mistakes. So, Peter sees more mistakes in his world than other people see.

Alan has a chip on his shoulder. His angry countenance frightens others and makes them defensive. It appears to Alan that people are awfully sensitive. He comes on even stronger to combat this defensiveness.

The vicious cycles above are visible everywhere if you look for them. People respond to our demeanor. We either bring out the best in people or we bring out the worst. This chapter describes how our state of mind plays itself out in our relationships.

THE PUNISHMENT MYTH

Isn't it true that punishment and pressure are necessary to deal with a person who stubbornly repeats counterproductive behaviors?

THE GRAIN OF TRUTH

People struggling with habitual behaviors need some type of support.

THE CHANGE OF HEART

You just lost a big order and probably a promotion because you had an argument with a customer, again. You are upset and embarrassed. You have been in this unpleasant situation before. You wonder why you always end up like this. You don't feel secure enough to admit you are troubled. You are even less likely to admit that you might have contributed to the problem. The people around you are upset with your behavior. What type of treatment do you want from others right now—humiliation, punishment, criticism, anger or pressure? Probably not. Understanding and restored faith in you probably would be your first two choices. Those are the attitudes that bring out the best in you, too.

Pressure and punishment worsen counterproductive behavior. People with destructive habits are feeling insecure. What they need is understanding and support that will help them regain their bearings. Even behaviorists say punishment will not change the person; at best it will only change the person's behavior. Self-esteem, confidence, wisdom and understanding are what allow people to drop destructive habits and make sound decisions in life. All of these qualities are brought out by goodwill, not by pressure and humiliation.

HOW WE BRING OUT THE BEST OR WORST IN PEOPLE

The Heisenberg Uncertainty Principle in physics states that the act of observation changes the matter being observed. Absolute objectivity is therefore impossible. This principle can be applied to human relations: your state of mind alters the behavior of people around you. The way people act around you depends on which of the following two interaction cycles is triggered by your state of mind.

Each cycle starts with thoughts. If John has positive thoughts about Gerry, then John has warm feelings toward Gerry. When he feels warm and respectful toward Gerry, he will bring out the best in her. When approached with goodwill, people listen more openly and respond more cooperatively. Even when an issue is sensitive or negative, a positive internal feeling leads to a productive discussion. Thus the adage, "What goes around comes around" applies to communication. The goodwill of each party brings out the goodwill in the other parties to create a positive rapport cycle.

On the other hand, if you are feeling irritated at someone, you will find yourself in a negative frame of mind and your interactions with people are likely to be unrewarding. When you are in a chip-on-the-shoulder state of mind, you think in terms of pressure and intimidation. Pressure and intimidation insult people and set up a battle of egos. People usually get defensive in the face of ill feeling. Thus, when you interact from feelings of irritation or anger you tend to bring out the worst in people, creating an ill will cycle. People instinctively know when someone has a chip on his shoulder and they bring out their defenses in response. They know enough not to allow themselves to be open to someone who is in a state of ill will.

Diagramed below are the ill will cycle and the positive rapport cycle. State of mind is the prime mover in both cycles.

NEGATIVE THOUGHTS
ILL WILL
↓
THE CHIP-ON-THE-SHOULDER CYCLE

Doesn't Listen	Foot Dragging
Emotionally Reactive	Poor Performance
Defensive	Undermining

→

It is easy to see why people locked in an ill will cycle experience frustration and complain that people are difficult. When a person feels ill will, he or she is living in a world of active egos and rigid personalities, with scant opportunities for progress and learning.

POSITIVE THOUGHTS
RAPPORT
↓
THE BENEFIT-OF-THE-DOUBT CYCLE

Listen Openly and Well	Creative
Flexible	Cooperative
Magnanimous	Peak Performance

→

When a person feels warm and respectful, the above dynamic occurs. He brings out the best in others who know his heart is in the right place. They listen openly, egos at rest, and return respect and warmth by putting themselves out for that person. Progress and learning are built into this dynamic. The positive rapport cycle maximizes teamwork and minimizes interpersonal friction.

A CHANGE OF HEART—THE VEHICLE FOR INSTANT CHANGE

Human beings have a miraculous ability: we can change our minds. We all can shift from a negative, judgmental perspective to a positive outlook without any change in circumstances. For lack of a better name, let's call this phenomenon a change of heart. A change of heart has the following characteristics:

- It takes a person from a negative, evaluative stance to an appreciative stance.

- It creates such a complete change in perspective that the person has trouble relating to the way he saw things only minutes earlier.

- It can happen any time, without warning. People are often surprised by it.

- A change of heart is preceded by a moment of truth.

The following chart shows how different the same thing looks before and after a change of heart. The change in perception provides us with a change in feeling. Before a change of heart, our view is critical and our feelings are therefore negative. After a change of heart, our view is appreciative and we feel grateful. Simultaneously, the nicer feelings generate more positive perceptions, thus creating a positive spiral.

Before a Change of Heart	After a Change of Heart
Bob is a difficult person.	Bob is a "character."
Life is turbulent.	Life is eventful.
That person is annoying.	That person is endearing.
Our house is old.	Our house has character.

A change of heart is always preceded by a moment of truth. Just before change occurs, our thinking quiets down to allow a moment of inner silence. In this moment, we see life anew; our old thinking drops away and we can take a fresh look at our circumstances.

The moment of truth may be anything from a subtle, unnoticed moment of clarity to a profound, moving experience. Heart attacks and near-death experiences often provide dramatic moments of truth that cause life-changing shifts in values and perspective. A quiet walk in the park or a moment of reflection over the breakfast table might lead to gentle, subtle moments of truth. These moments let us seen beyond our normal perception to insights. People who understand the insight process count on these quiet moments for guidance in life.

Quiet Mind → Moment of Truth → Fresh Look at Life → Change of Heart → Positive Outlook

A change of heart is a very common experience. The example that follows depicts a typical change of heart.

THE MAN ON THE PARK BENCH

A man was slumped on a park bench. He was despondent about his life. His job was boring. His children were difficult. His car was getting old. Even the park was dreary. He stopped thinking for a moment and relaxed against the back of the bench. Suddenly, he noticed the sound of birds singing. Feelings began to well up inside him. His face lit up. He became energized. Things began to look different to him. He changed his mind about the things that had bothered him earlier. He was competent at his job. He could clearly see all the love he had for his children and could overlook their occasional shortcomings. Even his car looked like a classic rather than a clunker. He felt very grateful that there were parks in the city that provided a place for such powerful moments of reflection.

All that is needed for a change of heart is a momentary quiet mind. The man in this story moved from a negative to a positive state of mind without the slightest change in circumstances. Positive feelings are so basic to our nature that they fill our minds whenever there is the slightest amount of room.

Change of heart is the mechanism for saving and improving relationships. It enables a marriage with a painful history to achieve a permanent new footing overnight. A change of heart by one party, however slight, is usually enough to create a positive spiral in the evolution of your relationship.

REACTION SPIRALS—HOW WE CAN SHORT-CIRCUIT THEM

If we interact when we feel insecure, our insecurity creates distortions, misinterpretations and misunderstandings. Often, both parties overreact to each other's words and deeds. I refer to these distorted interactions as "reaction spirals" because we are reacting out of emotion rather than wisdom. Ultimately, this leads to positions we later view as indefensible. An example of a common spiral follows:

THE DOWNWARD FEELING SPIRAL

> Jill feels insecure. She mistakenly thinks she would feel secure if Jack put himself out for her. She makes demands with that logic in her mind.
>
> Jack reacts to Jill's insecurity. He defends himself by emotionally withdrawing from her.
>
> Jack's withdrawal triggers more insecurity in Jill. She reacts aggressively seeking more intimacy with Jack.
>
> Jack reacts by withdrawing even further.
>
> Both end up feeling alienated, misunderstood and victimized.

A compassionate response to another's insecurity sets a positive spiral in motion. The domino effect, as illustrated in the following example, leads to closeness and health.

THE UPWARD FEELING SPIRAL

> Jill feels insecure. She mistakenly thinks that she would feel secure if Jack put himself out for her. She makes demands with that logic, in her mind.
>
> Jack reacts to Jill's insecurity. He defends himself by emotionally withdrawing from her.
>
> Jill realizes she is insecure, laughs at herself and gets her bearings.
>
> Jill sees Jack's withdrawal as a manifestation of his insecurity. Her heart goes out to him.

Jack sees Jill is insecure and responds with warmth and compassion.

In the face of her compassion, he relaxes and becomes more intimate.

In the face of his warmth, she calms down and regains her emotional bearings.

Both people feel understood and closer.

THE GOODWILL SCALE

The feeling state that you present to people hooks either their ego or their altruism. The following scale shows how different levels of cooperation response correspond to your different states of mind:

- If you are in a state of angry indignation, others will fight you tooth and nail.
- If you are in a state of annoyance and irritation, others will drag their feet.
- If you are in a state of contentment, others will join you.
- If you are in a state of appreciation, others will put themselves out for you.
- If you are in a state of deep gratitude, others will pull out all the stops to help you.

As your level of goodwill rises, people become ever more cooperative.

People are like magnets, either attracting or repelling each other. If your partner seems resistant toward you, you should notice whether you have lost your warm feelings towards him. Once you clear your head, you will feel the warmth return and he or she will respond in kind. Thus, the Biblical enjoinder holds true: "As you sow, so shall you reap."

BRINGING OUT THE BEST IN A CHILD

Martha and Bill Samuels came into counseling because of their concern for their 15-year-old son, Eugene. The Samuels had been unsuccessful in their attempts to get him to go to school. The counselor asked to meet alone with the parents first.

Bill. We've done just about everything and we can't get Eugene to go to school. We've punished him, yelled at him and even locked him in his room, but he's just too stubborn.

Therapist. Why doesn't he want to go to school?

Bill. Aw, he's lazy. He'd rather go goof off with those bums he calls friends.

Therapist. Is that what he told you or what you're surmising?

Bill. It's obvious. What else could it be?

Therapist. What about you, Martha? Have you talked to Eugene about his feelings about school?

Martha. I've tried, but you can't talk to him. All he does is stay away from home as much as he can except for dinner. I told my husband maybe we should refuse to feed him unless he becomes more cooperative.

Therapist. I know this may sound simplistic to you, but people don't respond well to an adversarial stance. They take offense, as your son has done, and become very stubborn. It humiliates people to be punished and chastised.

Martha. What do you mean by an adversarial stance?

Therapist. I mean that you don't have a feeling of goodwill toward your son. You're not on his side right now.

Bill. Goodwill? Look how he's treated us!

Therapist. Now we're back to the old chicken-egg dilemma. You and your son are in a vicious cycle. You're bringing out the worst in each other. Does that make sense?

Bill. I guess it does make sense, but I don't think you realize how badly he behaves.

Therapist. You have to allow for a tremendous amount of distortion in cases such as this. See, you and Eugene have brought out the worst in each other. You are not as heavy-handed as you appear, and Eugene is not really as stubborn as he has been lately. Your reactions to each other have polarized your behaviors. Believe me, it's very common for people to move toward behavioral extremes when egos get involved.

Bill. That all sounds fine and dandy, but what do we do from here? That's the question.

Therapist. For one thing, you have to get out of an adversarial stance and get your heart in the right place. If you continue your battle with your son, he'll just dig in further. The ego is amazingly persistent. People will bite off their noses to spite their faces if they're committed to a battle of wills. I'm sure your son would rather count you as friends than as enemies.

Martha. He sure doesn't act that way.

Therapist. Don't judge him too harshly. Remember that all of your behaviors have been exaggerated. Think for a moment. Wouldn't you like to start all over as friends and work it out together?

Bill. I don't think that's really possible at this stage, do you?

Therapist. Absolutely. A relationship can always get a fresh start. Kids are particularly good at forgiving and forgetting. What about you, Martha?

Martha. We have nothing to lose. We're at a dead end.

Therapist. Let me have a talk with Eugene, and then I'll get the three of you together.

(Eugene and the therapist meet.)

Therapist. I know you've been to a therapist before. Have those experiences been a plus for you?

Eugene. Definitely not!

Therapist. Whatever your previous therapy experiences were like, I want to assure you I'm going to make our meetings a positive experience. I'll be nice to you. (Eugene does not respond.)

Why don't I guess at how the situation looks to you and later, when you feel more comfortable with me, you can correct what I've said. (Eugene does not respond.)

I know things have been pretty rough between you and your folks. I know that they have been hassling you, particularly your dad. I imagine the pressure hasn't helped. I know pressure and harshness are not the ways to get things done in a family. Neither is stubbornness. It is my job to teach your family how to get along so things work out for all of you.

Eugene. Lots of luck.

Therapist. I don't need luck, but I do need for all of you to be open and to listen.

Eugene. My parents have been to three counselors and things are still screwed up. Why don't you mind your own business? I don't want to sit in here and listen to you.

Therapist. This is my business. My business is helping families to get along.

Eugene. You are wasting your time with this family.

Therapist. Do you want your folks to treat you nicer, with more respect?

Eugene. Yeah, and I want a Corvette, too!

Therapist. I might be able to get through to your parents. Let's face it, Eugene, this is your best shot right now at getting things at least bearable with your folks. I don't figure you have a better thing going on than to let me try. You might say, "Who cares," but I have never seen a kid who wouldn't want to have a nice thing with his parents.

Eugene. Just talk to them. What do you need me for?

Therapist. You have not exactly been the ideal child, Eugene. Things you've done have made the situation worse. (Eugene does not respond.)

All I ask from you is that you be as honest as you can be and that you listen to what I have to say.

Eugene. Yeah, okay, I'll listen.

Therapist. What happened to you with school? Most kids go to school if for no other reason than it is too much of a hassle not to.

Eugene. I screwed up this year. High school was much harder than I realized. I got way behind really fast, and then I said, "The hell with it." It's too late now to start going.

Therapist. Did you talk to your folks about it?

Eugene. No! They would just think I'm lazy.

Therapist. Your parents could relate to someone getting discouraged and giving up. Everyone has discouraging thoughts sometimes.

Eugene. You don't understand. My folks can give other people a break but never me.

Therapist. Your folks want a fresh start with you. You know, drop all the hard feelings—hopefully get off on the right foot this time.

Eugene. Oh, sure they do. It's just a way to get me back to school.

Therapist. Did they learn their skepticism from you or did you learn it from them? (He laughs.)

Eugene. I don't know (smiling.) I guess I do have a bad attitude, sometimes. Starting over sounds good, but… I don't know. Maybe it's too late.

Therapist. Look, Eugene, all you have to do is forgive and forget all the crazy things that have been said and done. Pretend it's all a bad dream.

Eugene. Well, if they're willing, yeah, I'll give it a shot.

(The whole family now meets with the therapist.)

Therapist. Eugene is way behind in school. He doesn't see the sense in going back to school when he can't possibly catch up.

Martha. Is that what it is, Eugene?

Eugene. Yeah.

Martha. Why didn't you tell us that?

Bill. I think that's just an excuse. He should have thought of that when he let himself get behind in the first place.

Therapist. With all due respect, Bill, what you just said doesn't help the progress of this conversation. You had an impatient, negative edge in your voice. People are often offended by negative edges. They get defensive and respond in kind. Do you understand what I am suggesting?

Bill. Okay. I suppose I shouldn't be so pessimistic, but I am really discouraged.

Therapist. Your son, Eugene, got into the situation he's in today by reacting to his own discouragement. It's easy to be discouraged about a situation that has spiraled down like yours has. I'm sure you and your wife can easily get discouraged about it, too. But the only way to reverse the spiral is to look beyond the thoughts of discouragement to the possibility of a fresh start. When any of the three of you indulge in your discouraging thoughts, you run the risk of discouraging the other two.

Bill. Discouraged? I didn't think you cared enough to be discouraged, Eugene.

Eugene. Oh, man, I don't believe it. Of course I'm discouraged. I hate being one of the few kids not in school. I mean, for one thing, it's illegal. And, believe it or not, I wouldn't mind getting a diploma. It bums me out that you think I'm such a loser, and it bums me out that I'm always letting you down.

Martha. Why didn't you tell us these things, Eugene? It would have made a difference to us.

Eugene. I don't know. I didn't know you were interested.

Bill. I'm all confused now. What's the truth, anyway? Is the truth the way he was yesterday or what he says today?

Therapist. They're both truths, Bill. They're separate realities. When a person is insecure, as Eugene was, he's like a Mr. Hyde. His thinking is defensive, his behavior is habitual and he will react rather than respond. He'll live in a negative reality. When the person feels secure, he moves into a positive reality and becomes Dr. Jeckyl. He thinks with more reflection, like Eugene has done today, and he responds out of wisdom and foresight. We're all that way, actually. One minute Mr. Hyde and the next Dr. Jeckyl. The idea is to have a Dr. Jeckyl environment in your home. You create it with warm positive feelings. We've had that environment in this session for only a short while, and yet look at how differently you all see things and how differently you feel.

Bill. Is it really just that simple?

Therapist. Once you commit yourself to a feeling of goodwill in the family, the good feelings start to feed on themselves. You get better and better at helping each other out. You just have to trust that being in a goodwill reality will take care of external circumstances.

Bill. I can see I have to lighten up on Eugene. I still don't see what we can do about the school problem.

Martha. We can talk about it later, Bill. At least we can talk about it.

Eugene. I'll talk about it if you don't yell and threaten me.

Bill. I hope I don't end up yelling. I don't know if you can teach an old dog new tricks.

Therapist. You don't have to be perfect. It is reassuring to Eugene that you are trying to be supportive even if you don't always succeed. Isn't that right, Eugene?

Eugene. Yeah.

Martha. What a nightmare we've been through. Thank you for helping us take a new approach to things.

IN A NUTSHELL

- Notice your inner feeling, your state of mind, before you deliver a sensitive message. If you have a chip on your shoulder, get your heart in the right place. Look inside to find more understanding and compassion. Remember that everyone deserves to be seen in the most favorable light. When your heart is back in the right place, you will bring out the best in others.

- When you notice defensiveness in a listener, stop, wait and approach that person again with more gentleness and goodwill. That person will likely respond in kind.

10
DON'T DEAL WITH PROBLEMS TRANSCEND THEM

"I figure when we get through solving all our problems we will have a great marriage. But my friend told me if we have so many problems, our relationship isn't worth fixing. Another friend said if you aren't constantly solving problems in a relationship, you will be bored. Who is right?"

When I tell clients not to work on problems they look incredulous, as if I am telling them not to eat or drink. That's because everyone assumes that the only way to solve problems is to work on them.

Ironically, a focus on problems is the number one relationship killer. It lowers your spirits and makes things look worse than they really are.

There is a way to get where you want to go without focusing on problems. This way is so natural and effortless it doesn't look like you're doing anything. This chapter includes an account of a couple who approach life in this effortless way. In another case, we see how attention inflates problems in the same way worrying about a sore thumb will make it swell.

THE PROBLEMS MYTH

Isn't it best to deal with problems by discussing them up front whenever they bother one partner?

THE GRAIN OF TRUTH

A relationship needs a way to evolve and find solutions to the issues at hand.

THE CHANGE OF HEART

"Problems" don't really exist. They are mirages that appear to exist when certain conditions are present, such as an insecure state of mind. Problems are nothing more than situations seen through a filter of insecurity.

> SITUATION + INSECURE MIND-SET
> = THE ILLUSION OF A "PROBLEM"

Here is an example of how the problem mirage is created. Standing in line is something we all experience. You may be in line to purchase concert tickets or to check baggage at an airport. It can be an opportunity to take a break and maybe do some people-watching. If you feel time pressure, though, or have thoughts about how inappropriate it is for you to be waiting there, you may see the wait as a problem.

Relationship problems are issues that trigger emotional reactions from both partners. Were it not for these emotional reactions, the issues wouldn't be worth talking about because they would be resolved effortlessly in the course of living. Money matters, for example, are a problem for some couples and not for others. When finances are not a "problem," money matters take care of themselves. When the couple has money, they spend it. When they don't, they don't. If they disagree about expenditure, they discuss it. If the discussion is deadlocked, they assume the issue will resolve itself later.

When a couple sees money as a problem, the very thought of it fills their heads with reactions, and every exchange on the subject generates more reactive thoughts. The word "problem" brings on feelings of insecurity. "Problem" is, in fact, a state of mind that can focus on any issue.

If you have a sore on your arm, the last thing you should do is poke at it. Your doctor would treat the wound gently, creating the best possible healing environment. So-called relationship problems should be treated the same way. The thoughts around these issues trigger emotional reactions. If we are not careful, we will spend our time dealing with these emotional reactions instead of the issue. To treat an emotional sore spot, we should create a secure environment where the problem area can heal.

For every problem, there is a solution. Often there are many solutions. These solutions are usually obvious to the dispassionate observer, but we cannot see them when our minds are clouded by emotional reactions. When the emotional environment is no longer turbulent, we can calm down and access our natural wisdom. Now a discussion is productive, and will continue to be productive as long as the emotional sores are left alone to heal. If one of the parties irritates the sore—stirs up the other's thinking—the discussion will begin to deteriorate.

Once a couple sees how insecurity undermines the problem-solving process, they will have fewer unproductive discussions. Once they back off of problems, they will begin to have insights that yield solutions.

There are two basic human thought models: the problem mode and the solution mode. The problem mode is tedious and time-consuming. In this mode, people analyze, rehash, defend their positions and attempt to convert others to their viewpoint. When a couple or group uses the problem mode, they achieve a compromise "solution" that none of the parties really likes.

The solution mode is quiet and efficient. We clear our minds instead of filling them with details. We reflect, look and listen. Suddenly, out of nowhere, we get an insight. The insight comes with a feeling of exhilaration. When we see the solution, we can't believe we didn't see it earlier. The solutions we get from this mode are always so obvious that others readily embrace them. When a couple or group uses the solution mode, they end up feeling close, and they always reach a consensus.

People can fill their heads with problems or solutions, but we function better when our heads are filled with solutions. Faith is what keeps us in the solution mode—faith that there are perfect solutions to our problems and that those solutions will be visible once we calm down and take a fresh look.

PROBLEMS AS MENTAL QUICKSAND

Did you ever notice that problems are like fly paper? The more involved you get, the more stuck you get. Focusing on a problem in order to solve it, makes as much sense as pulling on the ends of a knot to untie it. Talking together about "our" or "your" problems is like a tug-of-war.

You can't solve another person's problem. He or she will disqualify any solutions you propose, the "yes but" responds. Your solutions won't fit within that person's thought system because there aren't any solutions there. That is why the problem is a problem. After you listen to people and their problems long enough, you begin to realize the problems lie in thought systems, not in the world. If you think you have a problem, accept that your thought system is giving you trouble, not the world. Think of it this way: if you can't fit into a pair of pants, the problem lies with your body, not with your pants. Our thought systems obscure the simple, obvious solutions to our problems. When our thought systems move to the background, we see the answers and say, "Why didn't I think of that before?"

Life's events and circumstances can be seen at many different levels of understanding.

How You See It	How You Will Feel
Catastrophe	Depressed
Problem	Stressed Out
Situation	Interested
Opportunity	Grateful
Windfall	Exhilarated

The possibilities and limitations you notice are a good gauge for your state of mind. If you see lots of possibilities, your head's in a good place. If your head is full of limitations, you are in trouble. Push escape, reset or whatever else will clear your mind. Possibilities will enter your head when you regain your sense of perspective.

SEEING ANSWERS TOGETHER

Tom and Sheila are in their mid-20s. They have been together for five years. Sheila would like to get married. Tom would prefer to live together. They came to counseling at Sheila's insistence.

Sheila. We've been together long enough. I want more of a commitment from Tom. I'd like us to get married.

Tom. I'm committed! I just don't want to get married. Marriage sounds so serious. Suppose things don't work out after we're married?

10 ♦ Don't Deal with Problems Transcend Them

Sheila. Why wouldn't they work out? Don't you like being with me?

Tom. That's not the point. The point is you never know what the future will hold.

Sheila. What is that supposed to mean? Do you know something I don't?

Tom. See how you're hassling me right now? I wouldn't want you to be pressuring me after we were married the way you are now. That's the kind of thing that makes me afraid to get married.

Sheila. (louder) I suppose you never give me any trouble.

Therapist. Do you see how quickly the feeling has spiraled down in the last few minutes? If you continued for another ten minutes, you'd be in divorce court.

Tom. Usually this discussion does end in the pits.

Sheila. That's for sure. We get a lot worse than this.

Therapist. See, the subject of marriages makes the two of you insecure. Whenever people are insecure, they have difficulty thinking clearly. Their thinking gets contaminated with negative emotions and thoughts, which make them more insecure, which hurts the quality of their thinking, which makes them more insecure and on and on. So a negative spiral is created. When two people in an insecure state of mind discuss an issue, they pass insecurity back and forth between them. The act of feeding on each other's insecurity exaggerates the downward spiral.

Sheila. I know this issue is a sensitive one to us. I also agree that we've never been able to discuss it fruitfully, never mind gracefully. But we do have to resolve this issue.

Therapist. Of course you want to come to a meeting of the minds on this matter. You always want to have deeper understanding in your relationship.

Tom. Of course. But what can we do to deal with this issue—or any sensitive issue, for that matter?

Therapist. To deal with sensitive issues, you must remain in a secure state of mind. When you are feeling insecure, you tend to take each other's comments personally. Your emotional reaction obscures your ability to see what is really being said. When you are in a secure state of mind, you see what is being said with perspective and understanding.

Tom. How do you make yourself feel secure?

Therapist. You clear your mind of negative thought and listen to what she is trying to say. As you gain understanding from the discussion, your level of intimacy increases and the shared understanding allows you to see the issue in a larger perspective.

Sheila. But I think if I saw how commitment looked to Tom, I might not like what I saw.

Therapist. You might not like it, but you would understand it. You would see that his reaction to commitment has nothing to do with you personally. It is just his idiosyncratic way of thinking. Besides, you'd be able to relate to the humanness of being restricted by your own thinking. You wouldn't look down on Tom, but would be compassionate. Tom would understand that from the way you see things, marriage would make you feel more secure inside. He might feel your hypothesis is wrong but, then again, he can certainly relate as a human being to operating on wrong hypotheses. These realizations would make you feel close. Does what I'm saying make sense to you?

Tom. You make it sound like there is something wrong with the way I view commitment.

Therapist. Your thinking is limited to you.

Tom. Why is commitment so good and necessary?

Therapist. Without commitment, you can't fully enjoy anything. Commitment frees you from the devices of your own mind. We are all the same. Our minds wander to indulge thoughts of possibilities, alternatives, concerns and doubts. Without commitment, we are likely to take these thoughts to heart and spoil our experience of the moment. Commitment keeps our eye on the ball so we can dismiss such distractions and return to enjoyment of the moment.

Tom. Are you saying I get distracted?

Therapist. That is not for me to say. What do you say?

Tom. I do think of alternatives and doubts, but doesn't everyone do that?

Sheila. I have those doubts, too, but I get over them as fast as I can. I hate to wallow in ambivalence.

Tom. (smiles) I guess I'm used to it. I didn't realize other people don't struggle with their doubts the way I do. I thought they weren't smart enough to have doubts and see alternatives like I did. (He shows some embarrassment.) Now you are suggesting I am the stupid one.

Therapist. You are the one suggesting that, Tom. We are just agreeing. (All three laugh.) We are all in the same boat. Life looks a certain way to us and we assume that's the way it really is. If you are ambivalent, your heart is never fully into what you are doing. Having distractions on your mind is like trying to relax while you are holding something in your hand. You can never fully relax because some of your attention is on keeping your hand closed. When you hold distracting thoughts like doubts and alternatives in your mind, you can't put your full attention on what you are doing.

Tom. I often start projects full bore and then lose interest. Doubts and alternatives creep into my head. Soon I am thinking more about those alternatives and less about my project. It never occurred to me that some people make a practice of dismissing those thoughts.

Therapist. That would be a good definition of commitment: dismissing doubts and alternatives in the name of enjoying your project or relationship more.

Sheila. I see the point you made earlier about understanding. I have that feeling of understanding for Tom when he describes some of his problems at work. I don't judge him. I just listen and try to help. Now that you mention it, I don't have any emotional reaction to what he says. I just feel closeness and understanding.

Tom. She really helps me when I am down about a problem. She makes me feel understood.

Sheila. I'd like to be able to listen that way about the commitment issue.

Therapist. It may be that right now that issue is too sensitive for you to discuss constructively. Tomorrow that might change. The point is to notice when you are taking it personally rather than listening with understanding. If that happens, stop the discussion before the negative spiral begins.

Sheila. But don't we have to discuss the issue of commitment to resolve it?

Therapist. No. In fact, most of the issues in life get resolved without discussion. They just take their course. Many couples never discuss commitment. They just get more intimate as time passes. At some level of closeness, they may decide that they want to live together. Later, it may occur to them to get married. It all evolves in an effortless, obvious way. If one of the two people had an emotional reaction to a step that they were contemplating, the other person would understand and they would come to some meeting of the minds. They would understand. They would have faith that as they got closer as a couple, their emotional reactions and insecurities would drop away.

Sheila. Tom, would you say you have certain emotional reactions and insecurities about getting married?

Tom. I do get a lot of crazy and confusing thoughts in my head when someone mentions marriage or commitment. I always have.

Therapist. Would you like to get beyond those reactions?

Tom. Absolutely. I know how much it means to Sheila to get married. I wish I could get behind the idea.

Therapist. All your distress about marriage and commitment is just some crazy thinking. It'll drop away at some point and you'll wonder why you made such a big deal out of the idea of marriage.

Tom. Sheila, do you think you might be a little crazy in your thinking, too?

Sheila. I love the idea of marriage but I'm a little suspicious that it means so much to me. I know you love me and the idea of marriage is hard for you. I see I need to be more understanding.

Tom. Me, too. I want to get over my reactions. I've been so busy defending myself; I haven't considered it any other way. I'm sorry I've been so resistant.

Therapist. Do you two notice you have that feeling of understanding now? You've been discussing the issue of commitment and marriage from a high state of mind. Do you see how easy and natural it is?

Sheila. It's funny, we didn't conclude anything and yet I feel more resolved about the issue. I always thought that only an increased commitment like getting engaged would satisfy me. I think I see now that an increased commitment would not satisfy me unless it was a plus for Tom, too. If it were an effort for him, I'd be insulted and it wouldn't mean anything. (She laughs.) I feel much less confused.

HOW "PROBLEMS" ARE TRANSCENDED

Bill and Wendy have been married fifteen years. They have three children: two boys, 11 and 12, and a girl, 18. This is his second marriage and her first. The interviewer had known the couple for eight years and was impressed by how effortlessly they got along.

Interviewer. Why do you two get along so well?

Bill. Because of her. (He laughs.)

Interviewer. Seriously. Many couples find it difficult to avoid friction. How do you two do it?

Bill. I don't know. Maybe we've been lucky.

Interviewer. Haven't you faced any adversity in your marriage?

Wendy. Nothing that came between us. We've had our share of hard times, but they made us closer.

Interviewer. Don't you have any problems in your relationship?

Wendy. I don't think so. We hardly have any friction if that is what you mean.

Interviewer. Are we dealing with a matter of semantics here? Is there another word you'd use instead of problems? Are you saying you see eye-to-eye on everything?

Bill. No. We see things differently in many areas.

Interviewer. Well, what do you do in those areas?

Wendy. We expect to have different views. We actually like that. It lets us learn from each other.

Interviewer. Aren't there important areas you disagree about? Aren't there issues where you wished the other person thought like you?

Wendy. Yes, there are some.

Interviewer. That's what most people mean when they use the word "problem."

Wendy. Oh!

Interviewer. Well, what do you do to resolve those areas, and how do you stay out of conflict?

Bill. We try not to deal with things head on. We let them sort of run their course.

Interviewer. Let's get specific. What is an example of an area of potential conflict in your marriage?

Wendy. Well, it looks like we won't be able to steer clear of these areas in this interview. (They laugh.) Actually, Bill wants to have another child and I don't.

Bill. Another area is that she always wanted to live in the country, but we've always lived in a city.

Wendy. That's right. I'm a country girl at heart. It would take me two minutes to get packed if we ever decided to move to the country. (They smile.)

Bill. Wendy has been very patient about that. I hope someday we'll live in the country.

Interviewer. Why don't you move now?

Wendy. It makes more sense to us to follow Bill's career opportunities than to pick the ideal location to live.

Interviewer. When you say "us," do you mean "us" or Bill?

Wendy. If I were living alone or with a man who looked at his career differently, this interview probably would be taking place in Oregon. (She smiles.) On the other hand, I can also see letting your career influence where you live. Bill loves his work and I'm really grateful for that. It seems a little crazy to me for him to give up his excellent work situation just to move to the country.

Interviewer. With all due respect, Wendy, don't you feel that you're making a sacrifice?

Wendy. Not at all! I have a wonderful life and Bill is no small part of it. I have a wonderful family, terrific friends and a beautiful home. We have as "country" a home as we can. Compared to how great my life is, where I live seems like a small detail. I feel so grateful for what I have; it's hard to get serious about the country issue.

Interviewer. What about having another child, Bill? Isn't that the kind of issue that can't be sloughed off?

Bill. Actually, I don't think about it unless I'm feeling kind of down. I can go weeks without it crossing my mind.

Interviewer. What about when you are down and it does bother you? What do you do then? Do you talk to Wendy about it?

Bill. Not usually. I just let it pass.

Interviewer. Why wouldn't you talk to Wendy?

Bill. Well, she's sensitive about it. I think she feels guilty because it means a lot to me and she wants to see me happy.

Wendy. Good guess, Bill. (She laughs.)

Bill. And because she's sensitive about having another baby, if I bring it up she'll probably get upset. It might even cause an argument. Then, for sure, I'll feel even worse. See, when we talk about a sensitive subject while we're both worked up, the chances of getting into a fight are pretty good. Nothing good will come from that.

Interviewer. Shouldn't you be able to talk about anything in your marriage? I assumed a couple with a good marriage could talk about anything.

Bill. We have learned from experience that we do better not talking about sensitive subjects when we're upset.

Interviewer. But, isn't it important in a marriage to be able to discuss sensitive subjects?

Bill. Let me put it this way. I'm an engineer. If you study any blueprint of a building, you can always see weak points in the structure. These points might be more than strong enough to keep the building up but they are definitely the weakest points in the structure, and you wouldn't want to put extra pressure on them. In fact, you would put as little pressure on them as possible. These points wouldn't hurt the general structure of the building unless you put undue stress on them. I think talking about sensitive areas when you're in a low state of mind puts unnecessary stress on the structure of the relationship. If we pile on enough stress, the relationship might collapse even though it's ninety percent sound.

Interviewer. I understand you don't tackle issues head on. What I don't understand is how you expect an issue to resolve itself if you don't focus on it.

Wendy. When we back off an issue, we put it out of our minds. Somehow it looks different the next time we think about it. I know my thinking has shifted considerably about the kids issue. Yet I seldom think about it. I'm much more open to the possibility of having another child now than I've ever been. At first, I kept remembering how much time and energy our children took. Now, I'm beginning to remember how much fun we had bringing up our kids. My perspective is definitely changing.

Bill. My thinking has been changing, too. I don't feel as desperate when I think we might not have another child. As Wendy and I feel closer to each other, the issue seems less important.

Wendy. Who knows? Tomorrow morning I might wake up and insist we have a child. (She laughs.)

Interviewer. Thank you for such an enlightening interview.

IN A NUTSHELL

- There always comes a time when an issue becomes easy to talk about. Every situation gets "ripe."

- When you think or talk about an issue and your feeling of well-being drops, you should back away from it. A low mood will handicap your thinking and increase your susceptibility to emotional reactions.

- There is an obvious answer to every problem. Being too close to the problem is the reason these solutions are not apparent. That's why consultants can instantly see solutions to problems that clients have struggled with for years.

- A problem does not look like a problem when it is seen in the right light. It looks like a portrait of circumstances, or even an opportunity.

11
THE SOURCE OF CONFLICT
NO ONE WILL EVER SEE THE WORLD YOU SEE

"I am entering my 60s. When are people going to realize my view of reality is the only correct one?"

Probably the most pervasive and destructive habit in the world of relationships is the tendency to disagree. What makes more sense is seeing alignment, truth and consensus in the ideas of others. This chapter is a crash course in how to see and benefit from opposing viewpoints.

THE CONFLICT MYTH

Isn't some amount of fighting or arguing always part of a healthy relationship?

THE GRAIN OF TRUTH

We might entertain occasional antagonistic or judgmental thoughts about our mates.

THE CHANGE OF HEART

Antagonistic thought need not be acted out through arguing or fighting. When negative thoughts are taken in stride, they will not affect the relationship adversely. Understanding resides midway between thought and action. When we understand that thoughts have no power without our will, we can easily keep them from dictating actions. The progression from thought to behavior is a function of our level of understanding. In marital disputes the progression is usually as follows:

THOUGHT →	FEELING →	BEHAVIOR
thoughts of disagreement	feelings of defensiveness	argument or fight

Some couples see themselves fighting and have no idea how the fight started. Others see that their insecure or defensive feelings lead them into an argument. Still others see that thoughts of disagreement tempt them to feel bad and argue. The earlier in the process you see what is going on, the more opportunity you have to avoid a negative result.

All couples have occasional thoughts of disagreement, but these thoughts never have to lead to harsh words. The secret is in understanding how thought manifests into behavior. A couple with a deep understanding could have any number of different viewpoints without any interpersonal conflict.

A MEETING OF THE MINDS

Disagreeing is not something that automatically happens when you listen to opposing views. It is something you do in your mind. Disagreeing is a way of thinking. The opposite of disagreeing is understanding. Disagreeing involves comparing your old thinking to what's being said. When you act out the thought process of disagreeing, you argue. When you act out the thought process of understanding, you become more intimate and attain a meeting of the minds.

Depending on your state of mind, your reaction to "conflicting" viewpoints can range from horror to delight. You may be:

- Horrified at the ignorance and stubbornness of others
- Fearful that other people might impose their misguided views on you
- Bothered that others don't see the truth
- Irritated that others have different viewpoints
- Interested in the fact that we are all different
- Grateful that we can learn from each other
- Amused
- Delighted

HOW PEOPLE DEAL WITH OPPOSING VIEWS— THE OPTIONS AND THE RESULTS

BLOCK AND CENSURE THE OTHER PERSON'S OPINION

This is the most dysfunctional way of dealing with separate realities. You do everything in your power to stifle opposing opinions in the hope that they will disappear. We all know how some countries try to do this through censorship. But censorship often leads to an underground resistance that can become formidable. When parents use this strategy with their children, the children may run from home or create a "secret life."

STRONGLY OPPOSE

You allow the person to express his or her differing opinion, but you attack it with all your forces. Your strategy is to put up so much resistance that the person will choose to keep his opinions to himself. In a marriage, a partner employs this strategy by putting down the spouse whenever a view is expressed. Victims of this strategy seldom retreat under attack, however. Usually opposition strengthens people's resolve to have their views respected.

ARGUE

The intent of this strategy is to change the other person's view. The assumption is that if you could show the other person the logic that supports your view, he or she would drop the faulty view and adopt yours. The problem is, the other person also has a logic, which supports his or her view as strongly as your logic supports yours. Arguing polarizes viewpoints. Often you end up supporting a position you don't even agree with just for the sake of being "right." Egos do not allow us to discuss things constructively.

ACCEPT OR ALLOW FOR DIFFERING VIEWS

Using this strategy, you simply accept that we all have different realities, without judging or assessing, just as you accept certain laws of physics such as gravity. This position allows the other person to express his or her view without opposition. Stated views tend to evolve. When you get a clear view of your opinion, you will usually improve upon it. Expressing the ideas in a friendly forum lets people examine what they think and learn from the process. If the environment is adversarial rather than receptive, the person is defensive, unable to learn and ever more rigid in that view.

WELCOME AND RESPECT DIFFERING VIEWS ("CULTURAL EXCHANGE")

The most productive strategy in communicating is to learn from other views. When tourists go to foreign countries, they often assume the posture of students. They treat foreign customs with respect. They learn the secret of taking afternoon naps from the Mexicans. They learn to eat *sushi* and *sashimi* from the Japanese. They pick up fashion tips from the French. Separate realities within the same culture can offer similar learning opportunities. There is always a grain of truth in every view that opposes yours. The difference between accepting and welcoming differing views is measured in the amount of respect accorded to others' opinions. The more respect the better the response. Others make that extra effort to express themselves. They become better listeners. The rapport that results from this strategy creates a high level of intimacy.

When you feel compelled to argue, you know you are momentarily insecure. If you were secure, you would feel comfortable having opposing views. When you feel the internal pressure to disagree and argue, it is time to regain your internal bearings and remember that arguing is more likely to lead to polarization than to solutions.

I KNOW HOW TO RAISE KIDS!

Gerry and Karen have two children: a 4-year-old boy and a 10-year-old girl. The couple came into counseling because they argue bitterly about how to raise their children.

Karen. I just can't believe what Gerry lets the kids get away with. I expect Judy to do the dishes before she goes out. He tells her to go and he'll do them for her. How is she ever going to learn responsibility?

Gerry. You're so hard on her. I wanted to give her a break that time. We had eaten late and she wanted to go out with her friends.

Karen. That time! Every time is that time. Those kids play you for a fool. They walk all over you.

Gerry. They walk all over you, because they don't do what you tell them. They find any way they can to rebel. At least they do what I say when I ask them to do something.

Karen. Yeah, every blue moon is when you ask them to do something!

Therapist. Did you two ever notice the other person always has an answer to your argument?

Karen. What do you mean?

Therapist. I mean that you two could argue forever without resolution. Isn't that true?

Gerry. It has been true so far.

Therapist. Everyone has a different set of beliefs. Each person's set of beliefs could be called a belief system. All belief systems are self-validating and inclusive enough to provide an answer for every argument. When any two belief systems do battle, it always ends in a draw.

Gerry. Do you think we are incompatible?

Therapist. If having different belief systems meant couples were incompatible, then there would be no compatible couples. Every person has a different thought system. No two people see life the same way. Each person has his own "culture," so when any two people live together, you have two cultures under the same roof. Does this sound true to you?

Karen. You mean there is no man who sees parenting the way I do?

Therapist. You might find a man who had similar views. You will, however, disagree on some parenting decisions. The quality of your teamwork as parents depends on how you respond to differences of opinion. If you respond well to them, different points of view are not a problem. If you respond counterproductively, then differences of opinion lead to conflict and stress.

Gerry. I can see how we are bound to see things differently. What I can't see is what to do about differences in our parenting philosophy. Don't we have to find some common ground to parent together? What do couples do about separate viewpoints or separate cultures, as you called them?

Therapist. There are several positions couples can take concerning separate realities. The central issue is how each treats the other's opinion. There are many strategies you can adapt toward opposing opinions: stifle it, argue, consider, welcome.

Gerry. How do we apply these strategies to our situation? How am I supposed to learn from someone with such distorted views?

Therapist. Well, I can see from your comment that you are not quite up to the cultural exchange level yet. You have to look at the truth in what Karen is saying rather than what you disagree with. Karen understands children need some limits, some structure to guide them.

Gerry. I know, but…

Therapist. Gerry, you are about to argue, aren't you?

Gerry. Yes, I was. It bothers me that she thinks the way she does.

Therapist. Just listen and you'll get some respect for her thinking. You might even be able to learn from each other.

Gerry. I suppose you're right. She always says I'm a lousy listener.

Therapist. Karen understands that children need guidance and firmness. She reacts to you when you give in to the children in a moment of weakness. She thinks this creates a bad model for them. Does that make sense?

Gerry. So far it does. I know I shouldn't go overboard to please them like I sometimes do, but I'm reacting to Karen's rigidity. I also know it doesn't work to base my treatment of the kids on my reactions to Karen.

Karen. I'll have to admit I'm too harsh and overbearing sometimes, Gerry. I respect that you're more patient and more forgiving.

Therapist. You are beginning to get respect for each other and to examine your positions. Can you see how the discussion is progressing with the stance you're taking now?

Gerry. Sometimes I feel like the two of us are the blind leading the blind.

Therapist. Each of you has a tremendous amount to contribute to your parenting relationship. Karen, you are grounded in setting limits and teaching the children responsibility. Gerry, you are grounded in the realization that whatever is done with the children should be done with the right spirit. If you respect each other more you can learn from each other.

Karen. Gerry always wants things done in the right spirit. Even though I disagree I appreciate that he insists on things being nice for the kids. I was brought up in a family that was pretty grim and serious. One thing that attracted me to Gerry was his commitment to happy endings. I realize how I had begun to take that for granted. I have tried to make him more hard-nosed instead of learning to be more flexible myself.

Gerry. Could you talk to us about dealing with specific subjects, like chores? Should we require the children to do chores?

Therapist. Chores help a child learn responsibility and contribute to the family. Chores must be administered in the right spirit, though, or they lower the child's self-esteem and foster a bad attitude about responsibility.

Karen. That makes sense.

Therapist. I could go through every parenting issue and it would boil down to the same thing. Everything you said about each issue would include a personal component from your individual thought system and a common sense component from your deep wisdom. If you listen for what you disagree with, you'll hear the personal belief component and end up arguing. If you listen for the truth in what the other person says, you'll hear the common sense component and learn from the interaction.

Gerry. It sounds too simple.

Therapist. It is simple!

Karen. Gerry, let's talk about chores, and we will see what happens. I want the kids to take some responsibility. I don't want to spoil them by having them lounge around while you and I bust our backs to keep up the household.

Gerry. Spoiled! Those kids are hardly spoiled. They are nice, appreciative kids...

Therapist. You can see how innocently a person can fall into the habit of focusing on the disagreement in what is being said, can't you?

Gerry. I don't know what you are talking about! (Wife laughs.) I know what you are saying, but what should I do about misstatements I think she is making?

Therapist. Brush them aside so you can see the valid point she is making. The foundation of mutual understanding is built on this.

Gerry. What was the point?

Therapist. Karen, why don't you repeat what you said.

Karen. I want the kids to contribute to housekeeping. We work hard enough as it is. I don't want to spoil them.

Therapist. Gerry, do you feel that the kids should contribute to the housekeeping? Do you feel that you two work hard? Do you think it would be a mistake to spoil the children?

Gerry. Of course I agree with those statements. Is that what you mean by looking for what I agree with?

Therapist. Exactly.

Gerry. That's simple. Now what?

Therapist. Now just respond to those statements.

Gerry. Well, I don't want to spoil the kids, and yet I don't want to oppress them and take the fun out of their lives.

Karen. Oppress them!

Therapist. Remember now, the point is to find a meeting of the minds, not to look for the weakness in what has been said.

Karen. Well, I certainly don't want to oppress them either. We should just make sure we are not asking too much of them.

Gerry. Our oldest, Judy, has a lot of homework. I think we should consider that when we plan for her chores.

Karen. That is a good point. But, she doesn't have homework now, in the summer.

Gerry. I agree she should have more chores in the summer.

Karen. We don't expect our son to do anything, because he is so young. If the idea is to get help and keep them from being spoiled, we should find something he can do. It would be good for him to feel that he is helping.

Gerry. He could at least pick up after himself in the living room.

Karen. He could help me with chores around the house.

Gerry. You could say to him, "Michael, it is time for you to help me," so he sees he has a job, too.

Karen. Good idea.

Gerry. I know! Let's each make a list of what we think each kid should do. Then we will go over it and see if we think they can do each thing. We will make sure we are not giving them too much.

Karen. I think some things we have asked them to do have been too much for them. I ask Judy to clean up after dinner and she does part of the job and splits. I should break the job down and do part of it myself.

Gerry. I do feel we should go over the list with Judy.

Karen. Good idea. We might ask her about the chores we have set out for her brother. She knows what he can do.

Gerry. It will be good for her to help us to make up Michael's chores. She will have to think from another perspective.

Therapist. You two have definitely picked up the gist of what we were discussing.

Karen. It was easy. It's just different from what we are used to doing.

Gerry. I like it. It made me feel close to Karen.

Karen. I feel so much freer. I think better when I know Gerry is going to try to understand what I am trying to say.

Therapist. Everyone finds it nicer to reach a meeting of the minds instead of a stalemate.

IN A NUTSHELL

- Realize that arguing and fighting are not productive. The insecurity in a conflict environment minimizes learning.
- See different viewpoints as an opportunity to understand each other better.
- Listen for the truth in what the other person is saying when there is a difference of opinion. The other person will find it easier to communicate in a non-adversarial atmosphere. You will find yourself learning from each other.

12
EXIT EXCITEMENT, ENTER LOVE
LEVELS OF RELATIONSHIPS

"The excitement phase is winding down. It's time to learn to fight so we can keep the relationship interesting."

Many, if not most, marriages do great during the honeymoon phase (six months to eighteen months). It's when the newness and excitement wear off that the "troubles begin." This pattern leads people to conclude that marriages, like consumer goods, have built-in obsolescence. Not so! Couples just don't understand how relationships evolve.

THE STALE MARRIAGE MYTH

Don't most marriages eventually "grow stale?"

THE GRAIN OF TRUTH

If relationships don't evolve and deepen, they do tend to get stale.

THE CHANGE OF HEART

As marriages evolve, they quiet down. They get deeper rather than more stimulating. More stimulating, is like a back scratch. Deeper is like a back massage. Deeper is more satisfying but less dramatic. It seldom occurs to people that the reason they seek so much excitement is that excitement is not very satisfying.

A couple's sex life reflects this principle during the first two years of marriage. At first, sex is the major source of intimacy in marriage. As the relationship evolves, intimacy comes more from sharing and companionship than from sex. These more subtle forms of intimacy are also more profound. An "I love you" over the phone, or a moment of silence together after the kids are in bed, can leave one with a warm feeling for hours. Intimacy becomes more than an experience limited to the bedroom.

Couples who don't appreciate what deepening is become concerned when their relationship quiets down. They think something's wrong. They worry they aren't as sexually active and don't pursue excitement as much. This concern creates unrest in their minds and, thus, in the relationship. Unrest lowers the intimacy level. Now, they have neither excitement nor intimacy.

They need to see that as a marriage quiets down it becomes more fulfilling. The partners feel more relaxed—more themselves—in each other's company, dropping even the most subtle pretenses. They become more open to life and to each other. They get more enjoyment with less effort. They become more appreciative. When it is time to be out in the world, they are more rested and refreshed. When a couple acquires a taste for contentment, they truly appreciate the deepening feelings in their marriage.

LEVELS OF RELATIONSHIP

CONFLICT LEVEL

Both parties are poisoned by anger and insulted by the treatment they are receiving. They also feel insecure and off-balance, which brings out their worst. There may even be physical fighting and the relationship may feel raw and numb. Communication is difficult and usually makes things worse. A jump in the level of understanding brings hope, patience and temporary peace.

COPING LEVEL

The good news at this level is that the fights can be kept under control. The bad news: maintaining control is a full-time job. The relationship feels unpleasant and strained, burdened by judgments and expectations. Surprisingly, feelings of superiority and guilt often occur simultaneously. Partners find themselves worn out from the constant demands of "handling" the relationship. Communications are strained and warm feelings are scarce. A jump in the level of understanding helps develop compassion and goodwill.

COOPERATION LEVEL

Planning, coordination and compatibility are achievable at this level because goodwill is present. Both parties trust the good intentions of the other and view counterproductive behavior as innocent and fueled by insecurity. They give each other the benefit of the doubt. Where incompatibility and lack of alignment exist, good communication and mutual support fill the gap. A jump in the level of understanding here provides greater faith and trust.

SYNERGY LEVEL

Problems, stresses and incompatibilities don't even appear at this level. Individual differences are buffered by feelings of appreciation, respect and gratitude. Being together energizes the parties. They talk less and share more positive feelings. This level brings out the best in everybody. A jump in the level of understanding brings even deeper feelings.

SOUL MATES

You carry the other person in your heart at this level. The couple feels strong kinship and intimacy—as friends, lovers, working partners or family. They want to spend as much time together as possible. Their shared moments have a timeless quality—a little bit goes a long way. A jump in the level of understanding leads to even more depth of feeling.

LEVELS OF RELATIONSHIP—AN INTERVIEW

Barbara and Michael have been married for eleven years. They were selected for this interview because of their high level of rapport.

Interviewer. How long have you two been together?

Barbara. Eleven years.

Interviewer. It seems to me that marriage would seem old and uninteresting after a while.

Michael. Like after ten years or so? (He laughs.)

Interviewer. Now that you mention it, yes.

Barbara. Before I got married, I wondered if we would get bored.

12 ♦ Exit Excitement, Enter Love Levels of Relationships

Interviewer. Well?

Michael. (laughing) Hardly! Barbara is more interesting and more enjoyable to me than ever.

Barbara. That's sweet.

Interviewer. What have you done to keep your relationship interesting?

Barbara. We haven't really done anything.

Michael. It seems to me our relationship has gone through stages that have kept things interesting.

Interviewer. What are these stages?

Michael. We don't really know. I would be making them up just to answer the question.

Barbara. That sounds like fun. Let's see if we see them the same way.

Interviewer. I just want to get some idea of what you mean. Maybe it will take away my concern that marriages get stale.

Michael. Well, the first stage for us was not very pleasant. I will call it the stage of fighting.

Barbara. I would call it hell. Actually, Michael, the first seven or eight months were fun. It was very exciting. We enjoyed the physical part of the relationship. We loved to party and do things together. I was really enthralled with the novelty of having a mate.

Michael. That excitement wore off at some point, didn't it?

Barbara. Yes, it sure did, and afterward, we were both a little disillusioned. We tried to make it exciting again— we couldn't. Then I started thinking, "It's time to evaluate Michael as a prospective mate." I started looking at you closely and I didn't like much of what I saw.

Michael. Enter the fighting stage. We both criticized what we didn't like in each other. We looked for possible problems.

Barbara. When Michael went out to a ball game with his friends, I thought, "I don't need a mate who leaves me alone." But he had gone out with his friends before and I didn't give it a thought. Now it was the beginning of World War III.

Michael. Everything became an issue to us.

Interviewer. What happened? How did you last ten years?

Michael. We wouldn't have lasted ten years if our marriage hadn't turned around. We went to a marriage counselor who knew what he was doing. He helped us to straighten things out.

Interviewer. What did he tell you?

Michael. He suggested we stop trying to analyze and "work on" the relationship and concentrate on enjoying each other.

Interviewer. I can't imagine that to be practical advice. How could you be expected to enjoy each other given how bad you felt about each other?

Michael. I didn't think it was practical either, but somehow it worked.

Barbara. It gave me permission to enjoy Michael. I could enjoy the relationship, even though we had not gotten it together.

Michael. I can't tell you how quickly the relationship started to improve. I am not saying it was perfect overnight. But, it did turn around overnight. It is quite different being in a relationship that is getting worse each day than being in one that is getting better. It really made us feel relieved and grateful to see this change.

12 ♦ Exit Excitement, Enter Love
Levels of Relationships

Interviewer. What was your relationship like after that point?

Barbara. We got along.

Michael. That says it all. I guess that would be the next stage—compatibility.

Barbara. By compatible I mean the amount of tension and conflict decreased dramatically. We fought less and less.

Michael. When we did fight, the fights didn't last as long. Isn't that true, Barbara?

Barbara. Absolutely. They were fewer and farther between.

Michael. There is another difference. Before we learned how to get along, we never got over a fight completely. During the conflict stage, we would be left with a residue, a scar. We secretly kept score. If memory serves me right, I was the one most wronged. (Laughter.) In the compatibility period, we got over each fight completely. Every fight was forgiven and forgotten almost immediately.

Interviewer. Your relationship in the compatibility stage sounds ideal: a few short fights, no scars. That must be the last stage? I would settle for a relationship like that.

Barbara. If you had asked us earlier, we would have settled for it too.

Michael. The next thing that happened was we got used to each other. We were more relaxed around each other. Things suddenly got easier. We got closer. With these feelings of closeness, we weren't tempted to fight.

Barbara. When we reached what could be called the "comfortable" stage, we saw in retrospect why we had trouble breaking our habit of fighting—fights were appealing because they were familiar. They created excitement and it was always fun making up. Now we weren't tempted to fight because our everyday feeling was about as good as the feeling of "making up."

Interviewer. Why were you suddenly feeling so much closer?

Barbara. I began to relax more and be myself around Michael. Before then, I was still having mild emotional reactions to what he said and did. It's hard to relax when you have those thoughts.

Michael. Feeling comfortable around Barbara made our relationship a paradise. We could discuss anything without fear or conflict. We didn't have to talk all the time. Before, I felt obliged to engage her in conversation.

Barbara. I used to feel the same obligation to keep up a rapport. I thought it was part of the marriage contract. Now I don't feel we have to talk all the time. It is nice sometimes being together quietly.

Michael. We are really best friends now.

Barbara. You're right, Michael. We are best friends! There is no one I would rather be with than you. There is no one I would rather talk to, either.

Interviewer. Weren't you always best friends?

Michael. Not really. We were careful around each other. We got along great but we didn't get along easily. I was always a little guarded about Barbara. It was stressful. It was only a little tension, but tension it was. We occasionally needed a break from the tension. We felt the need to go out with our friends or spend some time away from each other. I'm not saying that is wrong or that we wouldn't do the same thing now. I am just saying when you need to escape, the relationship isn't quite right.

Barbara. I could spend all day and night with you now without wanting a break. That was not always the case. Come to think of it, I didn't really think of you as a friend then. I thought of you as my husband. Now, I think of you as both.

Interviewer. This might sound stupid but wouldn't you get bored being so comfortable?

Barbara. That is not a stupid question. I had exactly the same concern before I experienced the nicer feelings.

Michael. I did too.

Barbara. The feelings you get when you feel super-close to someone are so satisfying that boredom is not an issue. I don't think anyone could ever get sick of those deep feelings of well-being and closeness.

Michael. I thought to myself, if we don't argue or talk about "important issues," what would we do with our time? We found we spent the extra time having fun and fooling around. We joke just the way I used to joke with my fraternity buddies. We seem to laugh at everything. It keeps us in good spirits.

Barbara. That is one great benefit of having a nice feeling with your mate: as soon as you get home, your spirits get raised. You forget your day.

Interviewer. I trust the comfortable stage is the last one.

Michael. Not really. We don't really know what the last one is. That is the nice thing about a relationship evolving. You never know what is next.

Interviewer. Would you say that the comfortable stage is the best stage you two have gone through?

Michael. We recently experienced another jump in closeness. This stage is harder to talk about. I am not sure we could do it justice.

Barbara. I want to hear about this.

Michael. Do you know how it is said that if a person lives with a pet for a long time he begins to look like his pet?

Interviewer. Don't tell me you are starting to look alike.

Barbara. God forbid! (Laughs.)

Michael. We are starting to think alike. We seldom disagree. She is always thinking one step ahead of me.

Barbara. That's true.

Michael. I feel closer to you than I have ever felt to anyone. I carry you in my heart. When someone mentions your name, a warm glow comes over me.

Barbara. You are sweet, Michael. I have noticed the same thing and I didn't know what to make of it.

Interviewer. How is this feeling different from being best friends?

Barbara. The comfortable feeling was wonderful and this is a dream come true. This feeling I have for Michael is the feeling I dreamed I would have for my mate.

Michael. I feel that way, too. I can't imagine being without you.

Interviewer. Can you identify what helped you go from one level to another?

Michael. I don't know. It just happened.

Barbara. Maybe wanting the good feelings and thinking they are possible helps. Unless we were told, we didn't realize the path was heading always toward warmth and affinity.

Interviewer. Thank you for your honesty. This interview was very touching. I would like to find those same feelings in my marriage.

Barbara. Believe me. If we can get along after the rocky start we had, anyone can do it.

HOW A RELATIONSHIP EVOLVES—AN INTERVIEW

Tom and Helen have been married for twenty-two years. They were selected for this interview because of their high level of rapport.

Interviewer. How long have you two been married?

Helen. Twenty-two years.

Tom. We got married in college.

Interviewer. How did you meet?

Helen. Tom was my brother's best friend in high school. I met him when I was eighteen.

Interviewer. Was it love at first sight?

Helen. Second or third sight would be more accurate.

Tom. Fourth or fifth sight would be more accurate for me.

Interviewer. I noticed you get along well. You seem to enjoy each other. Is that the way it has always been?

Helen. We have always enjoyed each other's company, haven't we, Tom?

Tom. We've had some good times for sure.

Interviewer. I know this is putting you on the spot, but do you get along as well now as you did when you were first together?

Helen. Better. We're much closer now.

Interviewer. Would you agree, Tom?

Tom. Definitely.

Helen. Our relationship is different now.

Interviewer. In what way?

Helen. When we were first married, we were in love with being in love, if you know what I mean. Our relationship was exciting. We were getting to know each other and we went to football games and parties. We were active all the time.

Interviewer. How long did that excitement last?

Helen. Six months to a year. I don't remember exactly.

Tom. It was a year and a half. I remember exactly because I was disappointed when the excitement wore off. I was afraid that things would go downhill. I had nightmares about this tired, old, boring couple.

Helen. I didn't know you felt that way! Why didn't you tell me?

Tom. Because it didn't get boring. It turned out to be better than that exciting period. Didn't you have the same concern?

Helen. My parents' relationship was always alive and intimate. I just trusted that something good would replace the excitement.

Tom. My parents' relationship was one of the boring ones. Maybe that is why I was concerned. My dad used to complain a lot.

Interviewer. Helen, you said that you trusted that something would replace the excitement. What replaced the excitement?

Helen. Intimacy. A deeper intimacy. Looking back, I would say that our relationship quieted down, got deeper. Contentment replaced excitement. I felt more satisfied being with Tom. We started enjoying just being together. We didn't plan to go out less; we just tended to turn down invitations.

Tom. I would say we became friends after having been lovers. I mean we were still lovers but we were friends, too. Do you know what I mean?

Interviewer. What did you do during this so-called quiet period?

Tom. We talked less, did less and enjoyed each other more. We made love less. It was less of a big deal. When we did make love, it was much more satisfying. Yet, I would say that our romantic relationship was overall more gratifying. Doing less was more satisfying.

Interviewer. Why were you suddenly closer?

Helen. I don't know.

Tom. Me neither.

Interviewer. Is that the stage you are in now?

Helen. No. We are much more intimate now than we were back then.

Interviewer. Say more about that.

Helen. We see things the same. We operate at the same pace and appreciate many of the same things. We are more of one mind. We joke around a lot. We are like best friends now. I guess if you are fond of someone, you tend to get fonder over time.

Interviewer. Pardon my irreverence, but I would think that a mate would get predictable and boring over twenty or so years.

Tom. Helen is a different person than the woman I married. Watching her has always been interesting to me. It's been like being married to several different women.

Helen. That's true of Tom. There's no way he's the man I married.

Interviewer. Give me an example of what you would call a change.

Helen. Tom was a purposeful, focused person when I first met him. He wasn't much for shopping, the arts or lying out in the sun. Now he is a champ at lying on a beach for hours. He's really soft and relaxed. He is still effective in the world. He's a very successful lawyer. He is just well-rounded now. There are other changes, too. He is more thoughtful and more sensitive. He didn't know what being thoughtful was five years ago. He was a bull in a china shop. I overlooked that because I loved him. Then suddenly he became thoughtful.

Tom. Helen used to be serious. Now she is lighthearted. Early in our relationship, almost no one would seek her out as a friend. She was too up-tight around other people. Now everyone wants to be around her. She is a lot of fun.

Interviewer. Why do you think these changes came about? I know you are not psychologists, but what's your guess?

Tom. When you feel secure around someone, I think it is natural to let your guard down and relax around them. When we were first together, I put most of my energy into keeping my act together. That kept me the same. I figured she was with me because she liked the way I was. I was afraid if I let my guard down, she might not like me anymore. My efforts to keep my act together made it impossible for me to change. As I felt secure I started showing behaviors I didn't know I was capable of. I didn't know I could enjoy the little things in life, for example. I started noticing flowers, the décor of houses, what people on the street wore and hair styles.

Before, I hardly noticed the change in seasons. I didn't know I was capable of being observant in that way. That one change made my life so much more enjoyable.

Helen. And it gave us so much more in common. That's how our relationship became more enjoyable: every time one of us saw a new aspect of life, we could share more as a couple. For example, when I became more outgoing, our social life became more varied.

Interviewer. That makes sense.

Helen. I became more confident as time went by. There is nothing that brings out the best in you like someone loving and appreciating you. We had that from the start and I think it was good for our self-esteem.

Interviewer. Do you have any suggestions about how to have a long and happy relationship?

Helen. I can't think of any. It seems like our relationship got better on its own. We were lucky.

Tom. Marry a wonderful woman like Helen. That's the secret. (Laughs.) I do have one suggestion. When the relationship quiets down, it's easy to get concerned. I was even tempted to start fights to get the stimulation back into the relationship. It is reassuring to know the fallow periods are followed by a deeper, more satisfying level of intimacy.

Interviewer. You seem to be suggesting that when the relationship changes form, one has to be patient and not get insecure about the change.

Tom. That sounds better than what I said!

Interviewer. The difference is you live what you said and it's still a theory to me. I hope I can experience that same gentle evolution in my relationship that you found in yours.

THE LEAP OF FAITH

When we sit in a rocking chair at ninety-seven and reflect, we will see the sense in the evolution of our relationships. We can't see that sense now because the understanding we need to appreciate change only comes after the change is completed. You can't understand how a mystery turns out until you read the ending.

If the change in your relationship frightens or upsets you, it means you don't understand it yet. Once you do, you will appreciate and welcome it. This premise requires a leap of faith. But let's face it, most of life is like that. What we don't understand, we don't like. Perspective leads to understanding, which leads to appreciation.

If we learn to take leaps of faith we don't have to fight change until we understand it. We can enjoy it right away, knowing it will make sense eventually.

IN A NUTSHELL

- Respect familiarity and comfort in a relationship.
- Take the transitional periods in stride. During these periods, the relationship may seem old because the new experience of the relationship has not yet emerged. Those periods are a sign that a deeper, more satisfying way of relating is on the way.

13
IT'S NEVER TOO LATE TO GET A FRESH START

"I'll get back at her. I'll suffer the pain of resentment until she apologizes. When I get hurt, I hold on to the pain. I don't forgive and forget. That way, no one can ever hurt me because I am already hurt. I think I am onto something with this system."

Clients tell me they feel foolish being understanding and forgiving. "My friends say I should be upset with my wife. They see me as a wimp and a doormat." But these clients have forgotten that it hurts to be upset and to bear grudges. Anger and resentment are painful feelings. Why would it be smart to try to feel this way? An analogy to physical pain shows the logic. Suppose a friend put sharp rocks in her shoes because she didn't like what her husband did. You notice the rocks are causing bleeding and sores. Doesn't it make sense for her to remove the rocks and stop the pain?

This chapter suggests that self-inflicted emotional pain, resentments and grudges are just bad habits that make things worse by adding more insecurity to a situation. Forgiving and forgetting are the answer.

THE MYTH OF "THE PAST"

Doesn't the past doom some relationships? Isn't there such a thing as "too much water under the bridge?"

THE GRAIN OF TRUTH

Some couples get so discouraged by their painful memories that they give up.

THE CHANGE OF HEART

When a relationship has been troubled for a long time, the partners usually have accumulated painful memories that overshadow their feeling of love. When the feeling of love is obscured, they begin to view each other in a negative light that creates more unpleasant memories. This, in turn lowers the feeling level, which darkens their outlook further. This downward spiral continually lowers the level of goodwill between the partners. No wonder the couples get discouraged and want to throw in the towel. It is unreasonable to expect them to stay in their relationship under these circumstances. It would be asking a lot to want them to stay together, even if the spiral were to slow down.

For the marriage to be "saved," the spiral must be reversed. This is always possible. There is no such thing as a point of no return in a relationship. Relationships can always get a fresh start.

The cycle is reversed when partners empty the pool of painful memories from their minds. When the painful thoughts are gone, they will be replaced by warm, positive thoughts and feelings that lay the foundation for a fresh start. Forgiveness sets this process in motion.

Forgiving results from clearing unwanted thoughts from our minds. We forgive when we use our power of understanding to strip these thoughts of their negative charge. Once a memory is forgiven, it is easily forgotten. Forgiving and forgetting don't have to be learned or practiced; these skills are innate. To forgive and forget, you need only see that such action is possible and advantageous.

When a man learns his wife has an incurable illness, for example, he can drop a lifetime of negative memories in a matter of seconds. A person in this situation would be unlikely to say, "I know my wife has only a few months to live, but I can't be nice to her because of past resentments." If people can forget the past in emergencies, they have the power to forgive and forget at will.

People think of forgiveness as a generous act, but it is actually very self-serving. If you have painful memories, you suffer. They're like burrs that rub your skin every time the memories are simulated. Getting rid of the burrs so your wounds can heal is really being nice to yourself.

When we forgive, we come to peace with ourselves and the painful thoughts that have been sitting in our minds tormenting us. Forgiveness is the act of seeing those thoughts with understanding. Understanding lets us see the humanity of others and cast offending events in a more positive light. Understanding depersonalizes the event, transferring it from the "this is what happens to me" category to just another example of what happens in life.

When couples decide to forgive and forget, they relieve themselves of a tremendous amount of pain and begin a new life with new thoughts, new feelings, new possibilities and a new perspective on the past. A fresh start also leaves couples feeling warm and close. Partners look nicer, more well-meaning to each other.

HOW TO FORGIVE AND FORGET—QUESTIONS AND ANSWERS

Why would partners who have been unhappy for many years be motivated to feel warm toward each other and get a fresh start?

It makes sense to try again. In my counseling practice, I often mediate adversarial divorce property settlements. The first thing I do is help the couple to find a nice feeling toward each other. Without that goodwill, there's no chance for a settlement. In an atmosphere of ill will, the parties will pick any issue—no matter how petty—to act out their bad feeling. Sometimes the good feeling leads to more than an equitable settlement. When one partner suddenly feels warm toward the other, he or she often says, "I'm puzzled. Why are we getting a divorce?"

How do you get two people who hate each other to get to feel warm? That sounds totally unrealistic to me.

It is not unrealistic at all. All they need to do is have a change of heart. Everyone prefers to feel kindness toward someone rather than malice. People know deep down that it is bad to bear grudges and harbor resentment. I get the partners to realize how harmful it is to bear the pain they have been living with. I show them how much each would benefit from a warm affinity with the other. They would realize that habitual thoughts about their mates are ruining their fun in life and dominating their thinking. At some point the partners would commit to dropping the ill will and begin having positive feelings. They would be ready to get a fresh outlook on the relationship and see each other in a positive light. They would be open.

  I would then want the partners to see how distorted their relationship has been. People act out their insecurity by engaging in counterproductive behaviors. Others return tit for tat. Both personalities become polarized, exaggerated. A husband, for example, may react to his wife's pushiness by becoming stubborn. The wife responds with more persistence. Neither person's behavior represents the way he would act if he approached the situation with wisdom. When you see the distortion in your behavior, you'll notice the other person's behavior is also distorted—it may not represent his deeper intentions. Now both partners have reached a position of humility.

What the couple needs now is compassion. They need to see the innocence in each other's behavior, even in the act that launched the downward spiral of reactions. It's not always obvious just how innocent people are. People have to see for themselves that every misguided action is accompanied by an insecure state of mind. The more misguided the action, the greater the insecurity and fear. If you look into the miscreant's eyes instead of at his behavior, you will always see these negative feelings. If he had a sense of well-being, he would have the wisdom to see his actions as counterproductive.

At some point, the partners will see the other's innocence and their hearts will go out to each other. They will see themselves as unwitting players in a comedy of errors, and they will see their history in the light of understanding. They will feel warm toward each other.

Do you expect telling people to believe that getting a fresh start is so simple?

Any person can have such a change of heart. All it takes is a realization that occurs in the *silence* of one's mind. Insights are products of the heart, not the head. They involve seeing, not thinking. Being touched by an insight shifts your thinking and your outlook on life so you have a change of heart. A change of heart is always a fresh start.

THE POWER OF MEMORY

Humans have the ability to store memories and bring those memories to mind so vividly they seem real, in the same way movies and dreams seem real. You dream your wife is having an affair with the milkman. When you wake up, would you confront her and file for divorce? Laughter is a more likely response.

The past is no more real than a dream. Once an event is over, it becomes a mere memory. The past has only as much power as you give it through your thoughts.

If you and your wife harbor unpleasant memories you will be unhappy. You may think the past is at fault, but actually you are looking at life through dark glasses spotted with negative thoughts and feelings. Remember, the spots are on the glasses, not on the relationship.

HOW WE REMEMBER AN EVENT IS EVERYTHING

The way you feel when you remember an event has everything to do with your level of understanding. Consider the example of a man who has been turned down for a date.

RUINED MY LIFE

You link being turned down to every painful memory you ever had. "This is the story of my life. Women just don't like me. I'll never have a family." You recreate the pain of all those memories and feel horrible. You assume your intense unhappiness validates the importance of this one incident, and languish in the dark thoughts generated by your low state of mind.

LEFT A SCAR

You react to the event by limiting yourself—"I will never ask someone out again unless I am sure she will say yes." You blame the incident for limiting your future happiness and hold the memories in your head, where you feel the pain frequently.

THINGS HAPPEN

In the grand scheme of things, what does this incident matter? Everyone has his share of adversity. "Not every woman is going to say yes."

A TURNING POINT

Before that event you didn't have the opportunity to enjoy life as you do now. That incident opened your eyes to your limited perception of life. You see possibilities you never saw before. You also see self-imposed limitations for the first time. When someone says something that once triggered an emotional tailspin, you realize the tailspin was all in your mind. You used to protect yourself from other people. Now you don't have to live in a shell. Your life has opened up. You have a fond memory of the event and the people associated with it. "She reminded me that I could be more discriminating. I used to ask out anyone who I thought would go out with me."

BLESSING IN DISGUISE

You think of the event as a plus. Your inspired state of mind generates insight that helps your life even more. In retrospect it seems you "lucked out."

FORGIVING AND FORGETTING A PAINFUL AFFAIR

Anne came in to counseling because her husband of seven years, Nathan, had had an affair. They have two teenagers, both from previous marriages. She had heard about the affair two weeks earlier. Her friend recommended counseling because Anne was so depressed.

Anne. I've been so angry. I can't even look at him without getting upset.

Therapist. It must be very unpleasant around the house.

Anne. It is. Even the kids have noticed it. I just don't know what to do from here.

Therapist. As crazy as this might sound to you, you have to forgive him and remove that incident from your consciousness.

Anne. Are you serious? I will never forgive him.

Therapist. Do you see how troubled you've been lately?

Anne. I have felt terrible ever since I found out.

Therapist. You've been troubled because the thought of the affair has polluted your mind. That's what negative thoughts do to people.

Anne. It's not just a negative thought. It's a negative experience.

Therapist. It was an experience back then. It is just a thought now. The thought would be less troubling to you if it came from a dream.

Anne. But it wasn't a dream. It happened to me.

Therapist. It did happen to you, Anne. Nathan's affair was definitely a painful experience for you. That experience is now stored in your memory in the section called painful thoughts. If you dip into that section of your memory and bring those painful thoughts to mind, you will live in a feeling of distress.

Anne. What am I supposed to do? I can't get what he did to me out of my mind.

Therapist. Do you want to get that incident out of your mind? If you wanted to, you could.

Anne. I definitely don't want to forgive and forget. Why should I? He did a terrible thing.

Therapist. Forgiving and forgetting is a very selfish thing to do. You are the one suffering from the painful thoughts. Imagine you had a tight grip on a sharp rock that was cutting your hand. I suggest you drop it and you say, "I won't. I don't want to give him the satisfaction." Wouldn't you drop it so you would feel better? Resentments are like sharp rocks cutting into your psyche.

Anne. If holding onto resentments is such a bad idea, why do my friends do it? Everyone I know holds grudges, at least for a while.

Therapist. Some people have the mistaken idea that holding resentments somehow protects them from making the same mistake.

Anne. Don't they?

Therapist. No. They put your attention on the past rather than on the present. People make the same mistake over and over because they are distracted by their memories. They step into an open manhole because they are thinking about their problems instead of where they are going. The injuries from the fall just add to the problems.

Anne. I just feel a little foolish forgiving him. It is like I am condoning what he is doing.

Therapist. Are you afraid that if you forgive him your husband might think, "I guess Anne thinks it is all right for me to have affairs. She must think that if she has forgiven me."

Anne. I suppose he wouldn't really think that. But how could I forgive him even if I wanted to?

Therapist. First, you need some perspective. You have to see the affair in a more impersonal way. When people get unhappy, they do things they wouldn't normally do. Some people drink, some work compulsively, others feel sorry for themselves. We all have frailties that rear their ugly heads when we get insecure. Nathan acted out his frailty in an affair. It had to do with his state of mind and how he reacts to his insecurity. It really has little to do with you, personally.

Anne. When I get insecure, I don't have affairs.

Therapist. You get depressed and resentful, am I right?

Anne. I suppose.

Therapist. We all react to insecurity in our own innocent little ways.

Anne. What do I do about my marriage?

Therapist. Sometimes an incident like this wakes up a couple and gives them a brand new marriage.

Anne. Are you saying I should take him back?

Therapist. Wait and see. He might see things differently now. He may learn from the incident. You might reach a new understanding. When people act in a counterproductive way, as Nathan did, they are always insecure. He would never have done what he did if his thinking were right. It wouldn't have made any sense to him. Do you follow me?

Anne. Yes. That seems right.

Therapist. If you let your heart go out to him you'll see beyond his behavior to an insecure, confused state of mind. He might be as baffled by the affair as you are.

Anne. He does seem sensitive about it. I never looked at that sensitivity as insecurity.

Therapist. When you relate to his troubled state of mind, your compassion makes you feel warm toward him as it stills your insecurities.

Anne. I don't know if I want to get close to him again. I don't trust him.

Therapist. You must admit, the closer you two feel, the lower the odds of either of you having an affair. You always want to get as close to your mate as you can. Trust and security come from understanding. The more you understand him, the more you trust him. When you withdraw to protect yourself, you get out of touch with him and set yourself up for surprises.

Anne. Suppose I did feel compassion toward him? Then what?

Therapist. When people are troubled, they are sometimes more open. Incidents like affairs provide opportunities for deeper understanding. When you find that compassion you'll be in a good position to have a heart-to-heart talk with him. That talk will probably give you a new relationship.

Anne. I feel foolish taking such a charitable approach. How can I face my friends?

Therapist. When someone makes a mistake, you don't just write him off, do you?

Anne. That's true.

Therapist. You have to get your head in a good place to see the situation clearly. In your state of mind when you came in, you had trouble finding the chair.

Anne. I'm glad you have couch or I would have ended up on the floor.

Therapist. When you get an understanding attitude, you can have a fruitful talk with your husband. After that, when you reflect on the situation, you'll have some answers that will stand up on their own. Does that make sense?

Anne. It does. Every time I talk to someone I get different conclusions, which change again every time my mood changes.

Therapist. That's the good thing about tapping into your wisdom. What you will see will withstand your mood changes. You have to clear your head of an event to have access to wisdom. That is where forgiving and forgetting come into the picture. It is the first step in clearing your head.

ONE COUPLE'S FRESH START

THE HUSBAND'S STORY

The Rags. Everything was all right for about a year and then the relationship hit the skids. I don't know what happened, but suddenly she became critical and demanding. Why don't we spend more time together? Why do we have to live in such a small house? Why aren't you this way or that way? I didn't like being treated that way and I let her know it. That made it worse. In all fairness, we both seemed to do just the wrong thing.

The more she criticized me, the more I avoided her. Soon our disagreements turned into arguments and then fights, not physical fights, but loud shouting matches. I hated my feelings

13 ♦ It's Never Too Late to Get a Fresh Start

during those fights. We tried to talk out the issues, but they never seemed to get resolved. It was like putting together an automobile engine and ending up with a few extra parts.

As time went on, the issues seemed to increase. First, it was how we spent our time. Later, we would fight about money, friends and anything else we differed on.

We had been together a year and a half by now. The fights were longer and more frequent. I considered leaving the relationship. Although I thought seriously about splitting, I was too insecure to do it. I was afraid of being alone. My self-esteem was low. I felt I wasn't much of a mate if my marriage to April was so bad. I also got discouraged about relationships in general. I figured, "What is the use of getting out of this one if my next one might be just as bad?" I felt trapped, resigned.

April wanted us to see a marriage counselor. I was against the idea. I couldn't imagine how it could help and I didn't like that sort of thing. Finally, desperate, I agreed to go. At first, it looked like we would improve things through counseling. I got to air my grievances. I began to see patterns. April and I became more hopeful.

Our hopes turned to despair when we realized that identifying the problems did not solve them. In fact, the more we talked about the problems, the bigger they seemed to get. I got discouraged. I wanted to end the counseling, but April insisted we continue. We compromised by going to another counselor.

The Riches. This counselor was different. He was more of a teacher. The ideas he suggested sounded ridiculous to me at first. They didn't sound like bad ideas, they just sounded unrealistic. He suggested we forget our problems and start being happy together. He said the problems would take care of themselves if we got close. He taught us to take ourselves and our thoughts less seriously. He made it all seem so simple. I was skeptical, but there was no doubt

April and I started getting along better. The question in my mind was, "How long will the change last?"

Little did I know then that our relationship had turned around. Not only did we not slip back; we continued to improve. It appeared that April had decided to treat me better. She was more understanding. I felt better about her. It was easy for me to be nice to her.

It was as if she were a nicer person than before. I had more respect for her. I saw things about her I had never seen. I noticed, for example, that she was very observant of the world around her. She would point out beautiful houses and flowers. Instead of getting impatient with her for slowing us down, I began to enjoy seeing the world through her eyes.

April was a lot of fun. She was lighthearted. She didn't take life too seriously. She had a soft way about her. I found I was very relaxed and contented around her. It became easier and easier to be together. I looked forward to it. Although I didn't like her occasional criticisms, I saw that a fault is a small part of the big picture.

I hadn't expected to feel so much better about myself when I treated April better. My self-esteem was never higher. I felt like a good mate.

THE WIFE'S STORY

The Rags. When we first got married, everything was very exciting. But as time went on, I felt less appreciated and less cared for. There seemed to be so many other things in his life that were more important than me—his friends, his children, his work. I felt lost in the shuffle. When things calmed down and there was some time for the two of us, he was too tired or preoccupied to relate to me. I was insulted and resented the way I was being treated. We were supposed to be deeply involved and in love and yet I didn't feel loved. Out of my hurt feelings, I told him what I thought about his treatment of me. What I got for my efforts was more of the same. We started fighting.

I had recently gotten out of a long marriage and it was hard for me to admit to myself that this new marriage was worse. I just couldn't handle another defeat right now, no matter how bad the situation.

The Riches. We finally sought help. The second counselor who saw us suggested that we start enjoying each other instead of focusing on what we disliked about each other. My question was, "How is our relationship going to become the way we want it to be if we don't focus on it and work out our differences?"

It took a leap of faith to enjoy ourselves in the face of our "unhappy marriage." It was quite awkward at first. We had forgotten how to enjoy ourselves. We were out of the habit. But by then, I was willing to try anything, no matter how crazy it sounded.

Well, to my amazement, it worked. We started to get along. This calmed Steve down. It made him less preoccupied and more attentive. His attentiveness calmed me down and made me more secure in the relationship. I became warmer and less demanding.

The feeling in our relationship had previously spiraled down as we focused on our dislikes. The relationship was now spiraling up with positive feelings as we focused on enjoying each other.

The issues in our relationship changed in the light of our newfound feelings. Some issues just didn't matter anymore. The ones that mattered continued to make us fight. But we realized that we couldn't bear the bad feeling that came with the fighting. We had gotten so used to feeling good, we couldn't stand to fight anymore. We found the faith to let our differences work themselves out.

IN A NUTSHELL

- See the possibility of forgiving and forgetting.
- See how essential it is to your mental health to drop painful thoughts from your consciousness.
- Find the humility to see that you are both in this together.
- See the innocence you both possess.
- Remember that any relationship can get a fresh start today. That exhilarating feeling is always only a thought away!

14
INTIMACY
PLAIN AND SIMPLE

"Our form of intimacy is to be distracted together."

Couples say they want to be close, and they're relieved to learn that being intimate is not a matter of time or "deep" discussions. People have trouble appreciating the simplicity of intimacy. They expect it to be more difficult, more involved. The harder they search for intimacy, the farther off it seems. This chapter puts intimacy within everyone's reach.

THE INTIMACY MYTH

Doesn't intimacy require a large investment of time, talk and energy?

THE GRAIN OF TRUTH

When couples don't know where intimacy comes from, they have to exert lots of energy to get a little intimacy.

THE CHANGE OF HEART

Bob and Jan sit quietly at the candle-lit table. They have eaten dinner and dessert is on the way.

Jan. Why don't we ever spend any time together, Bob?

Bob. What do you mean? We're together right now!

Jan. I mean *together*!

Bob. How could we be more together than across a little table?

Jan. I know we are together physically, but I don't feel close to you.

Bob. I don't feel particularly close, either.

Jan. I know you went to a lot of effort to take me here tonight, Bob, and I appreciate that. I just don't feel your presence. It's as if your body is here and your mind is elsewhere.

Bob. I do have a lot of things on my mind.

Being intimate with others is the natural state. Intimacy is the feeling of closeness that comes when two people are together with nothing in particular on their minds. When one person gets absorbed in his own thoughts, however, the closeness will decrease. Closeness does not require time, conversation or effort. Couples who don't realize where intimacy comes from try to get it through emotional discussions or fights. To the extent that these discussions and fights clear the partners' minds, they provide moments of intimacy—the pleasure of making up. However, the fights are unnecessary. Those same moments also occur when the partners clear their minds and spend a few moments together with a high level of presence.

(SPAN OF ATTENTION) − (AMOUNT OF DISTRACTIONS)
= CAPACITY FOR INTIMACY

When a couple is first together, their intimacy level is usually very high because their focus is on enjoying each other. As they start evaluating each other (is this person "the one?"), they get distracted and their intimacy level drops. They attribute it to not being right for each other. They don't realize that the evaluation process itself is what dampened their intimacy.

Busy schedules and parental responsibilities need not affect the level of intimacy. If the partners focus on each other when they are together, their relationship will not lack intimacy. If, on the other hand, they think about tomorrow's meetings, they will lose their sense of intimacy. It is not the schedule itself that makes them less close; it is the thoughts about the schedule.

Being distracted is just a habit. Once you realize that some thinking is extraneous, your thinking will become more functional. Closeness takes care of itself as you gain more control over your thinking.

THE GOLD BEACH FEELING

Ron and Emily have been married for twelve years. They have five children ranging from six months to nine years of age. Emily requested counseling because she is unhappy in the marriage. Her chief complaint is that Ron is not intimate enough. Ron was willing to come in but didn't think they needed counseling. He was satisfied with the marriage.

Emily. I'm just not happy. We don't spend any time together.

Ron. Are you serious? I'm home every night and all weekend. I'd like to spend a few Sundays with my friends watching football, but you complain about the time so much…

Emily. You may be physically home but you're not really home. Your mind is always somewhere else.

Ron. Sure, I have a lot on my mind. I work hard.

Therapist. I think the issue here is intimacy. Many couples talk the way you just did. They don't understand what intimacy is and how to increase it.

Emily. Well, if we could spend more time together we'd be more intimate. Last summer when we went to Gold Beach on vacation, we got really close.

Therapist. Let me suggest to you, Emily, that it was not the amount of time that provided the intimacy. The amount of time provided Ron with the opportunity to clear his head of business thoughts. His clear head provided the opportunity for intimacy. Do you agree, Ron?

Ron. Yes, I did feel more relaxed on that vacation than I had in a long time. I actually forgot about work.

Therapist. Did you enjoy being relaxed and having nothing on your mind?

Ron. It was a little awkward at first, but I did enjoy it. I'm used to thinking all the time. At Gold Beach I hardly thought at all. I wasn't bored, either. The days were full.

Emily. We were so close at Gold Beach. I was heartbroken when we had to go home. I want so much to go back.

Therapist. The experience you had at Gold Beach is available to you at home. You two just have to learn to keep extraneous thoughts out of your minds.

Ron. I can't help being distracted. I have a lot to think about. I have a very responsible job.

Therapist. Wouldn't your performance improve if you could get a break from work every day?

Ron. I suppose. I just don't know if that's possible.

Therapist. If you look at three people in the same job, you'll notice they have differing abilities to leave their work at the office. Being distracted is just a habit. Do you see that, Ron?

Ron. It must be a lifelong habit because I've never been any different. My dad was the same way and my mom was always after him like Emily is after me.

Therapist. You're not thinking about work now, are you?

Ron. As a matter of fact, I'm not. I feel pretty relaxed here talking to you.

Therapist. Emily, do you feel the intimacy?

Emily. Yes, I do.

Therapist. And we're not even on Gold Beach. Ron hit the nail on the head when he said he was relaxed. Insecurity is what causes habitual behavior. When Ron feels unsafe or insecure, he lapses into distraction. When he feels secure he finds it easy to be in the moment. We're all that way.

Emily. What can I do to make it easier for him to be secure?

Therapist. When you pressure him about being more intimate, it probably makes him more insecure.

Ron. That's true. I feel guilty. My guilty thoughts are a distraction, aren't they?

Therapist. Also, Emily, you could offer more "presence" yourself. If you were more there in the moment, your presence would help to draw Ron out of his distractions. There is nothing like a strong human presence to draw a person into the moment. You probably notice that dynamic with your baby, right Ron?

Ron. For sure. When I get around him, I forget about everything. I can play with him for hours without a thought on my mind.

Emily. Are you suggesting I could be more intimate, too?

Therapist. I'm just guessing, based on what you have said that you probably have emotional reactions on your mind when you're with Ron. Probably your mind is filled with thoughts about how distracted he is and how much you miss the Gold Beach feeling.

Emily. Have you been sneaking around in my head? That's exactly what happens. I didn't see those thoughts as reactions, though. I saw them as appropriate.

Therapist. Ron views his thoughts about work as appropriate, given his job. It's the thoughts that seem appropriate and natural that are the main distractions. We take them for granted. That is why they persist. When we see them as voluntary, extraneous thoughts, they will begin to drop away.

Emily. I feel a little embarrassed. I'm down on poor Ron for being distracted and I'm just as distracted.

Ron. I thought the kids and the job were responsible for our drifting apart. That's why I thought it was a waste of time to go to counseling. Now I see our minds are responsible for our lack of intimacy. I guess we have to start paying more attention to how we think. It's good to know that the only problem is how we've been using our brains.

Emily. I sure feel closer right now.

Ron. Me, too. I feel like we have a second chance.

EASY INTIMACY

People who visit a foreign country sometimes rave about how close they felt to the residents. They are amazed to feel intimate despite the lack of a common language. I would suggest they found it easy to be intimate *because* they did not share a language. When we don't share a language, it is easy to experience our innate closeness.

If we are highly involved in an activity, we say we are "with it" or "there." At the opposite end of the spectrum we are "out of it." Consider watching a movie. At the lowest level of involvement, we are thinking so much about our kids, our schedule for next week, the temperature in the theater and so on that we can't even follow the plot. At the next level, we can follow the plot, but we're distracted by our judgments and comparisons. We are thinking about how the film jibes with the book, how badly an actor is performing or a mistake by the director. With all these distractions, it is hard to enjoy the movie. At a high level of involvement, we are so involved that we lose our sense of time and place. We are enthralled and touched by the movie.

The following is a more detailed description of levels of involvement as they apply to intimacy:

OBLIVIOUS

You are so absorbed in your thoughts you hardly notice the other person. He or she may feel insulted or awkward about your neglect.

DISTRACTED

At this level, your thoughts draw you away from contact with the other person. It is an effort to be fully present. The experience is unpleasant because it takes so much effort. The other person accuses you of not listening. You feel stressed and dissatisfied.

PRESENT

It is easy and satisfying for you to feel present with the other person. You are warmed by the contact. People say you are nice to talk to.

IMPACT

The feeling at this level is very strong. You are touched by the people you are with. Your mind is so free of distraction, you lose your sense of time. The experience is very rich. The person with you feels some chemistry with you. Your intimacy automatically deepens over time.

ONE MIND

Your mind is so free you understand each other with very little conversation. You feel so close to each other you would swear you have known each other longer than you actually have. This level just seems to happen and when it does, it is memorable.

IN A NUTSHELL

- Realize that any extraneous thoughts we have on our minds detract from our closeness to others.
- Begin to appreciate feelings of closeness.
- Remember that intimacy is a momentary experience that has nothing to do with time or conditions.

15
COMMITMENT
SELF-SACRIFICE OR SELF-SERVING?

"Of course I am committed. And I'm determined to stay in this relationship until it seems best for me to get out."

Commitment and intimacy are functions of our degree of mental involvement. The more engaged we are, the larger our capacity for commitment. Full involvement works out best for all parties. What limits our level of mental involvement is insecurity. When we indulge concerns, fears and doubts, we are too distracted to be fully involved. We are holding back.

Many clients see commitment as, at worst, self-sacrificing or, at best, a trade-off. In fact, commitment is very self-serving. When you see the logic behind commitment it is hard to resist the idea, but commitment is grossly misunderstood. This chapter will clarify and deepen your understanding of commitment.

SOME THOUGHTS ABOUT COMMITMENT

John stood in front of the movie theater. "Should I go or not?" he asked himself. "Maybe I'll go in and see if I like the movie." He bought a ticket and took a seat in the theater. "Looks like an adventure movie," he thought. "I don't know if I am in the mood for adventure. Maybe I should see what other movies are playing… I could go out to dinner instead… I saw that actor in a western movie. I didn't like him too much… I should have read the review before I decided to come… So far this movie isn't very absorbing."

There is no way that John can enjoy the movie with all the concerns, judgments and possibilities floating around in his head. John's enjoyment has been sidetracked by distracting thoughts. If he wholeheartedly and single-mindedly involved himself in the movie, he would have a chance to enjoy it. But he is experiencing his own errant thoughts instead. Commitment can be defined as a wholehearted, single-minded predisposition to a person or activity.

People make a commitment in order to enjoy someone or something, not because they already enjoy someone or something. Distraction and ambivalence tell you your commitment is weak. Commitment is a stance toward life, a predisposition to get the most out of each experience by dismissing thoughts and reactions that detract from its value.

Commitment to other people means seeing each person in the best possible light. To do this, we dismiss personal emotional reactions that might lessen enjoyment of others. The ultimate interpersonal commitment is to forgive and forget any residual thoughts that interfere with affinity and respect. Our special commitment to our mates requires us to dismiss adverse circumstances and emotional reactions.

Changes in mood and circumstances are bound to spark emotional reactions, concerns and speculations in a marriage. For example, you and your mate may have strong reactions to a financial setback. Indulging these thoughts injures both your rapport and your discussion. Commitment will help you take those thoughts in stride and maintain your closeness and respect.

The benefit you get from commitment is peace of mind on both sides. Your partner benefits from knowing you are committed to maintain respect and affinity. He need not fear that circumstance and personal reactions will hurt the relationship.

It is human nature for our degree of satisfaction to be tied to the extent of our involvement. Commitment prepares the mind for full involvement and guards against distractions.

Putting your whole heart into a relationship is the only way to get maximum value from it. Commitment to a relationship enables you to experience its full potential.

WHAT ABOUT PRINCESS CHARMING?

My wife, Linda, wanted a commitment from me right after we started living together. The whole idea made me nervous. What about Princess Charming? If she came along and I was already committed, I would miss the boat. It wasn't that Linda wasn't a nice person. It was just that she did not meet some of my specifications for Princess Charming.

Suppose she changed after we got married. Then what? What if I grew tired of her? I just wanted to wait until I was absolutely sure she would be the perfect mate forever. Until then I wanted to keep my options open.

I didn't realize how my lack of commitment affected Linda. She was insulted by it and lost respect for me. She also felt insecure when she thought I was still looking to leave her for Princess Charming. Her insecurity lowered her mood and made her less fun to live with. I held this difficult behavior against her and used it to justify my lower commitment. Neither of us realized what was occurring. We just felt we were not as compatible as we once thought we were.

I also didn't realize the effect my lack of commitment had on me. My observing, analytical state of mind kept my heart out of the relationship. It was hard to enjoy being with Linda from the distance I maintained.

Unwittingly, I put my focus on the problems and "defects" in the relationship. That made sense for evaluating the relationship, but it made no sense for enjoying it. I didn't realize my focus on shortcomings and problems was souring my perspective and compromising the experience. After a while, I had trouble seeing anything of value in the relationship.

By some miracle, Linda pulled us out of this spiral of discontent. She stopped taking my lack of commitment personally. She accepted my ambivalence. She said she felt compassion for me because I couldn't put my heart and soul into my experience of life. Linda's calm certainty and understanding rendered me defenseless. I had no choice but to consider what she was suggesting.

She also said she was totally committed to our relationship. She said she would make a point of being as nice to me as she could be, whatever my level of commitment. She said she had always dreamed of getting married and having a family. She hoped I would someday want that for myself.

In the ensuing weeks, I thought about what Linda said. I began to notice how some people wholeheartedly embrace their experiences in life and how others approach their experiences cautiously. I saw that young children always give life their all, and that when adults approach life the same way they seem to get a lot more out of it. They seem more vital. Commitment was no sacrifice; it was self-fulfilling. I saw the link between commitment and satisfaction.

These insights opened my mind to a different view of life. I couldn't believe how much mental energy I had spent on considering options, planning, second-guessing, regretting and doubting. I had never before noticed my extraneous thinking. Now, it was all I saw; it grabbed my attention constantly, and I wondered how I had ever gotten anything done with all that distraction.

15 ♦ Commitment
Self-Sacrifice or Self-Serving?

At this point, I saw my lack of commitment was a bad habit rather than a smart strategy. I saw that with all my distractions, putting my full attention on anything was, at best, an effort. I was beginning to see commitment's role in keeping all that wondering, evaluating and doubting out of my head.

I now had respect for those moments when I lost myself in an experience. I respected Linda's ability to be so involved in everyday activities like going for coffee and shopping. I was beginning to see my overlay of thought disappear now and then, and I noticed how much more engaging life was. Linda looked so much more desirable and fun in those moments. I felt so much closer to her. I felt younger, more relaxed. "I could be committed to this," I thought wistfully. I didn't yet realize that commitment was the only thing I needed to have these experiences all the time.

Linda and I got much closer over the next few months. She seemed like a different person to me and our relationship was so much better. I really enjoyed being with her. One day Linda came to me and asked to talk. Her delivery was gentle, but her message was a shock. "George," she said, "I can't get the idea of marriage and a family out of my head. I'd like to know if you want that, too."

"Are you saying you want to leave me?"

"No," she replied. "You're my mate. Do you want to be committed to me someday?" she asked. "I know your ability to commit yourself is the issue."

"I would like to be committed," I said. "I thought I didn't want to and then I found out I didn't know how." I suddenly felt sad.

Linda held me and said she was sorry to cause me such distress.

"If you appreciate commitment and want to live that way, I am sure you will get your wish. And when you do, I will be ready to arrange a wedding," she said with a smile.

Not a word was spoken about marriage or commitment until two months later, when I asked Linda to marry me. I woke up one morning and couldn't believe I was ever afraid of commitment. I could hardly relate to my previous fears. Commitment looked all positive to me—no sacrifices, no tradeoffs. I couldn't imagine why I thought there was a risk in wholehearted involvement, when it made life rich and satisfying. It now seemed ludicrous to consider what else I might do that could be better. I realized I had been caught up in a vicious circle: my dissatisfaction had motivated me to search for greener pastures and that search was the source of my dissatisfaction.

Linda honestly looked like Princess Charming. My job looked like Job Charming. I felt that understanding commitment was "growing up."

KNOCK-KNOCK—ANYBODY HOME?

NO ONE'S HOME

Consumed by problems and fearful thoughts, you are too preoccupied to notice, never mind enjoy, what's going on around you. You might have the idea you want a mate, but you really don't have enough positive thoughts to open a "relationship bank account." The problem is, you are taking your thoughts so seriously that you are lowering your well-being. As your level of well-being drops, you entertain more negative thoughts, and the downward cycle continues.

INDULGING YOUR CONCERNS

Fears, doubts and concerns are like flies that keep you from enjoying a picnic. Negative thoughts contaminate relationships.

Your concerns and fears will dominate your experience if you are too insecure to dismiss them.

FREE TO ENJOY

Although you have enough presence of mind to enjoy the other person, insecure thoughts stall the momentum toward intimacy. Examples of this level: you are dating a man and enjoying it, but thoughts of "Is he the one," or "Do I want a mate in this profession?" keep you from getting close to him. For married couples it might be memories of a fight or concern about "issues."

JUMP IN WITH BOTH FEET

You refuse to indulge in insecure thoughts that would keep you from enjoying the other person. You dismiss any negative thoughts. As a result, your involvement level is high enough to set a spiral of closeness in motion: you get more relaxed so that you feel closer, so that you enjoy the other person more, so that you get relaxed and so on.

SWEPT AWAY

The feelings of love and gratitude are so strong you think you have found "the one." This level evolves naturally from the "jump in with both feet" level.

16
SUMMARY

If there were a contest for the most simplistic clichés in the world, the following would be top candidates: "All you need is love"; "If you love each other enough, everything will take care of itself"; "Love makes the world go round"; and "Lucky in love." At the risk of losing credibility, I suggest that these sayings are absolutely true. Here's my supporting evidence:

- People in love see the beauty in life. Call them Pollyannas, unrealistic or optimists, but they get maximum pleasure from life today. When it looks bleak, they are hopeful about the possibility of a change for the better. When clouds appear, they are too busy watching the sun to notice, and when it does finally rain, they enjoy the change in weather. If they are caught unprepared, they laugh about it.

- A couple with a warm affinity bring out the best in each other. They treat each other like royalty and respond eagerly. Feelings of security subdue their egos and disruptive personality traits.

- A positive emotional climate elicits creativity and wisdom. A positive relationship makes geniuses and heroes out of ordinary people. The partners take this awakened intelligence out into the world with them. As these talents are expressed, confidence grows.

- Warm feelings in a relationship foster good teamwork. The better the feeling, the more productive the partners are together. "Synergy" is an advanced level of teamwork that allows partners to work as one. Working at a synergy level is effortless, efficient and invigorating.

- Couples with a high level of goodwill are insulated from adversity. Adversity brings them closer together and strengthens their bond. Goodwill makes it easy for them to correct mistakes in the relationship. They trust each other. When negative experiences occur, partners are grateful that negative experiences are an exception to them.

- The world responds positively to well-adjusted couples. People are more relaxed and generous with those who are secure and joyful. Their relationships appear to be charmed in the world. They seem to get more than their share of good breaks.

Having a loving feeling toward one's mate is its own reward. The fact that such feelings also enhance our functioning in the world is a bonus. There is no greater asset in life than positive relationships. Such relationships are available to anyone at every moment. What it takes to get there is a change of heart and the realization that when those feelings of warm affinity are present, everything else takes care of itself.

ADDENDUM

25 YEARS LATER

By George and Linda Pransky

PREFACE

It is hard to believe that *The Relationship Handbook* was written twenty-five years ago. At the time, it represented what I had learned about relationships since meeting the theosopher Sydney Banks in 1976.

Sydney Banks was the man who started it all, so to speak. He taught my wife, Linda, and me how to have a satisfying relationship. His wisdom was so effective that we dedicated our lives to teaching it to other couples. What you find in *The Relationship Handbook* is an accumulation of everything we learned through Sydney and through working with couples. What you don't find is the paradigm that Sydney discovered to describe his philosophy, the Three Principles. These principles are the center of our work and what we would like to share in this addendum.

Believe it or not, I have learned and experienced many things in these past twenty-five years. This retrospective addendum of *The Relationship Handbook* is like a giant postscript, a P.S. It is not like an auto manufacturer recall to fix defective understanding. The information contained doesn't contradict anything written in the original book. I simply see worthwhile things now that I didn't see before. Deeper, simpler things. This retrospective gives me an opportunity to capture and share that.

I considered rewriting *The Relationship Handbook* but thought it would interfere with the spirit of the book. I also considered writing a second book but thought there would be too much overlap of information. My solution: the retrospective addendum you see before you.

I asked my wife and business partner, Linda, to co-author this addendum with me. We took the most common topics people asked about after reading *The Relationship Handbook,* and we responded to each of them separately. We also included a vignette for each topic that spells out the logic in a coaching setting.

I want to thank our readers and clients for the belief they have in us and in what we teach. And I wish for everyone warm and meaningful relationships.

George Pransky

1
INTRODUCTION
WHERE IT ALL BEGAN

The field of psychology emerged out of a societal concern for those with troubled emotional states. In order to address this concern, psychologists have historically focused their energies and efforts on finding the cause of human feeling.

Here is a partial list of causes that have been "found" over the years:

- Genetics
- A bad childhood
- The weather
- The "wrong" house
- The "wrong" spouse
- The "wrong" lifestyle

Removing these causes, for example getting a new partner or moving to somewhere sunny, seemed to help some people but not others. Regardless, they were rarely long-term solutions.

In the 1970s, Sydney Banks was an ordinary man who had an extraordinary epiphany about the nature of life. That moment of truth cast a profound light on the nature of the human experience. He discovered that our feelings come directly and exclusively from our thoughts. Any feelings we have in any given moment will always reflect our thinking in that moment.

Many theorists had previously pointed to thought as a contributor to our experiences, but none had said what Sydney Banks said: thought is the *sole* contributor. Not lifestyle, not a spouse, not money problems, not conflicts, *just* thought.

If you pause and consider this, you will see that it is a no-brainer. If a person has positive thoughts, they will have happy feelings. If a person has negative thoughts, they will have bad feelings.

THE PRINCIPLES

Sydney's epiphany led to his formation of three vital principles of the human experience:

The Principle of Thought is that every person on earth has the power to create ideas, images, perceptions and memories within our own minds.

The Principle of Consciousness is our ability to form feelings from our thoughts. All of our feelings come from our thoughts.

The Principle of Mind explains that we are part of a larger, intelligent system. As part of this larger system, we can experience the power of new thought and, therefore, new experiences.

Understanding the nature of these three principles allows people to avoid chronic bad feelings. Here is how it works: thought is transient. Our thoughts are constantly changing. Even the same memory or idea will look different to us at different times of the day. Because of the ever-changing nature of our thinking, we can characterize thought as being illusory rather than fixed and solid.

Thoughts come and go uneventfully through our minds if we let them do so. When we fixate on a thought, it stays in our mind. Thoughts stick around according to how much importance we place on them. Chronic unwanted thoughts, and their respective feelings, are innocently held in place if we believe them to belong to external realities rather than being temporary and unimportant.

If you enjoy your partner and think she's wonderful, then that is what your thoughts are telling you. If you see beauty and goodness in your partner, then that is what your thoughts are telling you. It's no less your thoughts when you see faults and ugliness in your partner.

People sometimes ask me, "If both negative and positive thoughts are arbitrary, then which ones should I believe?" My answer is that the more you focus on shallow, unimportant issues, such as insecurities, habits, emotional reactions and irksome personality quirks, the more negative thoughts you'll have. But the more you see the true nature of human beings, the more thoughts you'll have about beauty and goodness. You have to decide for yourself: do you think that thoughts rooted in shallow, trivial observations are your truest reality? Or is your truest reality those thoughts you have that are rooted in something deep, sincere and fundamental?

When all is said and done, it's up to you to decide what thoughts to believe. This is your birthright.

THE BIG, BAD FIGHT

"Biggest mistake I ever made was getting involved with you. I don't know what I was thinking."

"I feel the same way. I could have done much better."

Linda and I shared those thoughts with each other on a long drive back from the airport at two o'clock in the morning after an international flight. We were tired and we were angry. We knew that being stuck in a car for hours would be problematic, yet we still allowed ourselves to buy into our moody thoughts. A lie detector would have affirmed that we were being honest about how we felt in that moment.

Luckily, Linda suddenly woke up to what we were doing. She realized that our thoughts had spiraled down, and we had said things that we would not normally say.

She said to me, "We are fortunate that we understand what we understand. Otherwise, that discussion alone might have ended up in divorce!"

She was right. Before we learned about relationships, those ugly words we said to each other would have left a permanent mark on our relationship. We would endure bad arguments all the time. Every time it happened we wondered if we were really meant to be together. We allowed those thoughts to take center stage in our relationship. In short, we allowed those negative thoughts to matter. We bore grudges, and as a result, our past weighed on us. It was like a heavy backpack that grew heavier over time. We loved each other, but our backs were getting weary.

We tried to talk about why we felt so negatively and what it would take to change things. All those discussions did was make us fixate more on our negative feelings, which added to our sense of hopelessness.

When Linda paused the ugly conversation we had in the car, she allowed us to both remember what we knew about thought. We remembered that our thoughts didn't have some special truth backing them; we didn't need to believe in them. It was reassuring to know that even with those extreme thoughts and feelings, we could come out unscathed and feeling warmly towards each other. It was encouraging that the turnaround was so fast. It was humbling to think that we could get that lost in our thinking but still feel so close afterwards.

I would categorize what happened in the car as the drama of life. Some couples' drama is more painful and difficult than others. This makes no difference as long as a couple can truly see the drama for what it is: thoughts that only exist as long as you buy into them.

2
THE THREE PRINCIPLES
THE CURE FOR RELATIONSHIP FAILURE

GEORGE'S TAKE

There is a generic relationship problem of couples generating unhappiness through their thoughts and blaming this unhappiness on the other person. They live in the illusion that the relationship is the problem. Then you have the generic cure: understanding how the mind works. When couples understand this it allows them to enjoy their time together. It is just that simple.

When clients first learn the Three Principles, they sometimes conclude, erroneously, that they just have to control their thinking so that they can create the positive feelings that they want. Unfortunately, that is not the case. Thinking comes so fast that we couldn't possibly control it! Luckily, we have two things going for us that don't require any action or effort on our part.

First, we have an innate wisdom which provides insight and new thought. No one is stuck in a certain mindset or idea. When we are in a good state of mind, we are in the best position to have new insights and new thoughts.

The second thing we have going for us is the fact that simply understanding the system casts our experience in a very different light. Rather than having our feelings imposed on us by forces beyond our control, our feelings are exclusively manufactured within our own minds. Knowing that fact allows us to take our thought-created reality less seriously.

THE OUTCOME

When Linda and I learned about the Three Principles, everything changed, yet it didn't. On a regular basis we still had fears, insecurities, jealousies and disagreements about parenting and finances. Yet something was different. These experiences would now come and go uneventfully. They no longer frightened us. We knew we could take them in stride, and we no longer gave them particular significance.

When our reactions to each other shrunk, or more accurately, didn't blow up, it was easier to see the love we felt for each other. Before, our emotional reactions were eclipsing all of our goodwill. After, we could feel the love even when we were in the midst of an upset.

When couples tell us the problems they have, Linda and I often realize that we have the same problems. Strong disagreements and hurt feelings are hardly out of our world. We accept that life will always be a full-contact sport. We realize that the answer to a nicer life lies in seeing "problems" for what they are: painful thoughts taken seriously.

We tell every couple that they don't have to change a life experience. They simply have to gain a different understanding about the life experience. The Principles are a perfect vehicle for doing that. Love and fondness are the default settings between human beings. When people realize that all they have to do is not buy into their emotional reactions, they will automatically land in love, emotional well-being and fondness. They will also see problems and issues in a different light. Either problems will seem less important or the couple will be able to tackle the problems with new ideas and renewed clarity.

LINDA'S TAKE

I thought that after I learned the Three Principles all of my relationship problems would disappear forever. Most humorously, I came to the conclusion that through this new understanding, George would become more like me. I thought this because I believed that I was already good at being in a relationship, and so the Principles would bring all of my "good-at-relationships" traits out of George.

In retrospect, the change that had the biggest effect on my life was the change that occurred within me. As I gained an understanding of how thought worked, I was able to see the effect my judgments and intolerance of George were having on me and my reality. I realized that I was dealing with myself and struggling with myself more than dealing with or struggling with George.

For example, George is a bit of a bull in a china shop. He is always accidentally breaking things and seemingly unaware of his surroundings. I used to hold this against him to the point that I wondered if I should really be with someone who was so oblivious. I now realize that my resentment came from my holding on to my judgments. It felt like it was my right to accept or not accept George's behavior. I eventually realized that this was such arrogant thinking, yet so many of my friends, family and clients did the same thing. Everyone was trying to change everyone else's behavior. The Three Principles allowed me to see that it wasn't George's behavior that was bringing down our relationship; it was my own thinking about it as some critical impediment to our happiness as a couple.

So how did this insight change our relationship? It's not like it made George or me change significantly in our behaviors, but it did allow us to be different and to accept each other's differences. And when we had problems that actually needed addressing, we were able to come to solutions easily. We weren't sidetracked by the stress of self-analyzing our relationship and having critical thoughts about each other. Problems became easier to discuss, and solutions to those problems became more readily available.

When I try to change George's behavior (which still happens), I'm able to wake up to what I'm doing and stop. If I'm in a really bad mood, it takes me longer to wake up, but I still do. And because we understand this phenomena, George and I don't take our arguments and criticisms to heart. We are very forgiving of each other.

THE CHICKEN-OR-THE-EGG SCENARIO

Lisa and Ron have been married for eleven years. They have a three-year-old son and a five-year-old daughter. They were referred by their minister who said that they are on different pages about many life decisions. He told us that their conversations go nowhere.

George. Your minister told us that you couldn't seem to agree on any life decisions. Is that true?

Ron. That would be an understatement.

George. Would you agree, Lisa?

Lisa. Ron just gets mad and walks away when we try to discuss things. If he would stick with it, we could sort things out.

George. Ron, do you want to stay together as a couple? Or better yet, how much do you want to stay together as a couple?

Ron. I don't want to stay together if there is going to be all this stress. When Lisa says I should 'stick with it', she means tolerate all the frustration that goes on during her so-called "discussions". Because we are so unhappy on a daily basis, I wouldn't want to stay together unless I had things my way. If we got along better, I would be willing to compromise where we live and our lifestyle.

Linda. We have a little bit of a chicken-or-the-egg scenario here. Or maybe it would be more accurate to say a self-fulfilling prophecy. All of your dissatisfied thoughts about where you live and your lifestyle are likely leading to feelings of unhappiness. Your unhappiness, in turn, motivates you to be insistent about your demands, and your insistence makes your conversations with Lisa more difficult.

Ron. So it's all on me? It's all my fault?

Linda. No. Lisa's thoughts are affecting her as well because she's feeling upset during your conversations. All the painful feelings both of you are having are coming from your own thoughts. That's the way it happens for human beings.

George. If you were to set aside your agendas of where and how you want to live, you would eliminate the fears and dissatisfaction that are plaguing your relationship. If the number one priority was to be happy in each other's company, you would use your thinking in a very different way. We are suggesting that you have the cart before the horse. You think that resolving your differences would make you happy as a couple. We are saying that being happy as a couple would resolve your differences.

Ron. Well, how do we find our happiness?

George. Happiness comes from good thoughts. If you have good thoughts, then you have good feelings.

Lisa. But even if we were happy individually and as a couple, wouldn't we still have to deal with our differences regarding how we want to live our lives?

Linda. Actually, you wouldn't have to "deal" with anything. If your mental well-being went to a higher level, many of the dissatisfactions that seem so important right now would lose their importance and their urgency. The issues that still remained? Working together, you would find the solutions.

Ron. You make it sound so easy.

George. For sure, it is simple. As you learn more about how the mind works, you will see how doable it really is.

3
GETTING OVER YOURSELF
WHY YOU NEED TO DO IT

"I don't understand why it's my responsibility to get over things rather than my partner's job not to upset me."

GEORGE'S TAKE

Early on in our relationship, Linda and I were both involved in the so-called "growth movement". We were deep into the "How Does That Make You Feel" approach and the "Working Things Out" approach. As a strategy, both of us tried to avoid doing the things that caused unpleasant reactions in the other person.

We became experts in what upset each other and used this knowledge to alter every aspect of our behavior. Believe me, it was a lot of effort to maintain, and it ultimately made things worse rather than better. Why? Because as we paid more attention to each other's emotional reactions, these emotional reactions became more visible, plentiful and important. We became more sensitive to each other, finding nonexistent distress in each other's tones and behaviors. We were like emotional hypochondriacs.

We couldn't connect the dots at the time. The strategy we were using was popular in our social circle. Everyone agreed that it was the best way to make a relationship work. Making matters worse, we were judgmental of the couples who were not sensitive to each other's feelings. To us they seemed like unenlightened brutes!

So what changed? We saw the possibility that we could get over our emotional reactions regardless of what it was our partners did to "trigger" them. We decided to stop worrying if one of us got upset, and we decided to stop trying to "fix it" when the other person had an emotional reaction.

The result was amazing! We realized that it was a lot less effort for us to get over our reactions than it was walking on eggshells around the person that we loved. It was a breath of fresh air that I could just be myself and not worry about what was upsetting Linda all the time. This doesn't mean I would intentionally do things to upset her, but when she did get upset it was not my responsibility to fix it.

THE GET OVER YOURSELF MODEL

By requiring your partner to be in charge of your emotional state, you are not only giving them an immense, impossible job, but also disregarding your own power over your thoughts, feelings and emotional reactions. The 'Get Over Yourself Model' makes life easier for your relationship. You don't have to spend time looking for your own sensitivities and avoiding your partner's sensitivities. You can accept that getting upset, or moody, or resentful is a part of the natural ups and downs of life and doesn't necessarily mean that something is wrong. Rather than holding on to upsetting feelings, you can spend your time enjoying your partner's company and relaxing into the relationship.

When you do get into an emotional reaction, it helps to notice that you have lost your bearings and that any unwanted feelings you are having are temporary. You can remind yourself that it is realistic and beneficial for you to get over your unwanted thoughts and feelings. Nothing wrong or bad is happening; it's just a natural part of being human.

You'll find that the 'Get Over Yourself Model' has a learning curve. You will get better and better at getting over your emotional reactions and returning to the well-being you had before the reactions occurred. You will also find that your emotional reactions will happen less frequently, for a shorter period of time and, most importantly, that they will take less of a toll on you when they do happen. In short, you will become more resilient.

I see getting over myself as not only beneficial to me, but in the service of the relationship. It isn't so much giving in, as it is not letting your mind get bogged down with negativity and emotional reactions.

LINDA'S TAKE

I used to believe that a person was committed to their state of mind and that it took time to change one's mind. This meant that when I got upset about something, I would either need the help of someone else to get over my emotional reaction or I would have to wait a long time to feel better.

Because of this, I often relied on George's compassion to get me over my emotional reactions. When he wasn't compassionate, I felt stuck in my negative feeling. I realized this wasn't working for our relationship. I had to start looking at things in a different way. So I looked at the negative thoughts that were causing my emotional reactions, and I asked myself what could be done about it. Could I possibly just get over my reactions by myself without the compassion that I'd always depended on? Could it be possible that I didn't need George to be a part of my recovery?

A DIFFERENT WAY

I was with my seven-year-old granddaughter one day, and we were in the middle of a huge disagreement. She was upset with me because I wouldn't buy her ice cream, and I was upset with her because she wouldn't stop whining about it. In the middle of this heated argument, she said to me, "Grandma, let's forget about it." In the blink of an eye she completely changed. She went from feeling angry to feeling completely neutral, and I was affected by it. I also went from feeling very upset to feeling neutral. With a big smile on my face, I said, "Sure." In that split second we were friends again having a really nice time and enjoying being together.

A BETTER STATE OF MIND

I didn't used to believe that a person could change their thinking mid-argument. I learned that when I am able to do this my entire relationship benefits, but, more importantly, it benefits me.

People are better at working things out through a better state of mind. Thus, George and I are always looking to get to a better feeling, not only because it feels better, but because we *think better*. When you feel better, you will have better ideas, better solutions and better answers. It's just righteousness, bullheadedness and attachment to a certain position that makes getting over yourself a struggle.

People often defend holding on to their anger because they think that if they are feeling *really* strongly about something, then they must be right. In reality, strong feelings just mean a person is having a strong thought, nothing more. No matter the severity, any state of mind or feeling can, and will, naturally change. I have to say that there is no perfection here, but there is learning and hope.

George and I are consistently looking for a better feeling in the middle of chaos. It doesn't always happen, but it happens enough. For example, sometimes in the middle of an argument with George, I will switch from defending myself or trying to prove my point of view, to suddenly not caring about being right. I love it when this happens because George stops being upset, and we both enter into a nice feeling. And when this happens it is much easier for us to talk through things.

If you get nothing else from this section, I would love for you to see the possibility that you can get over your emotional reactions, even mid-argument. Before understanding how the mind works, I never thought it was possible to have something change so dramatically between two people. All I needed was to see the possibility of change within my own mind, instead of looking to external circumstances and waiting for other people to change. It's not that circumstances and other people don't change; it's just that I found greater happiness when I stopped looking to the outside for direction and began getting over my emotional reactions on my own.

SEEING THROUGH EMOTIONAL REACTIONS

Bill and Susan have been together for five years. It has been five years of misery by their account, but they love each other and want desperately to stay together. They have been to countless self-improvement workshops and multiple therapists.

Linda. How would you characterize your problems?

Susan. We don't do well with boundaries, and I think he is very insensitive.

Bill. Therapists tell us that she is *overly* sensitive. She's angry and upset all day, every day.

Linda. Would you characterize yourself that way, Susan?

Susan. Yes. I know I'm too sensitive, but most of the problem is with how he treats me. He can be so heartless!

Bill. I am only that way with her because she gets nasty when she gets upset. That hurts my feelings and makes me lash out. In therapy, I discovered that getting angry is my way of protecting myself from her attacks.

George. I think you would be surprised to hear that many couples live in a frequent state of emotional reactions, whether they think of themselves as sensitive or insensitive. It's as common as crabgrass. People don't know how to fix their reactions. All they do is hope that the other person will change. Both people feel like they are hooked up to an emotional reaction machine, and the other person has the switch.

Bill. That's how it seems to me! (Susan nods.)

Linda. People don't understand where their feelings and emotions come from. It seems to them that emotions come directly from their partner's words and behaviors. They mistakenly think it's a fact of life, like bleeding when you are cut. In actual fact, all feelings, without exception, are generated within the minds of individuals via their thoughts. It is an inside-out system. Not outside-in.

Bill. I don't understand how you can say that! We tracked it in therapy, and we found that we only have those emotional reactions when the other person triggers them. Are you saying it's just coincidence?

George. You said that every time one of you has an emotional reaction, it is because the other person triggered it. However, you will probably notice that sometimes you don't react emotionally according to your usual patterns. There are exceptions. You may also notice that sometimes you react stronger than you do other times. Thus, your suggestion that there is a direct cause-and-effect is not true. It is just a statistical correlation.

Bill. So what are you suggesting?

George. When people think that their feelings are imposed on them by other people, they quite logically adopt this model: "We will refrain from doing things that cause reactions in the other person." Once people see that their emotional reactions are generated within their own minds via their own thoughts, they adopt another model: "I won't hold you responsible for my reactions. I'll just get over my reactions, and you get over yours." That frees them up to just live their lives and not have to walk on eggshells around each other.

Bill. I don't see how we can just get over our reactions. We never have been able to in the past.

Linda. Let's be honest, Bill. You haven't really tried to, because you didn't understand that your reactions were coming from your own thinking. It will be our job to teach you about how the mind works. You will see how human beings can naturally get over their feelings without having to work at it.

Susan. Is it really that easy? Have you dealt with couples as troubled as us?

Linda. We have dealt with couples much more troubled than you, and once they learned how their emotional reactions worked, they were able to get over their stress and distress on their own.

Susan. That is a huge relief to me, because it was so much effort the other way, and things were getting worse rather than better. This is like a light at the end of the tunnel.

Ron. I agree. I really love Susan, and I want to be with her. I can see that things could be good between us, and that is a giant relief.

4
PRODUCTIVE CONVERSATIONS
HOW TO MAKE IT HAPPEN

"I want to be able to discuss the tough stuff with my partner, but we always get too upset to continue."

GEORGE'S TAKE

Linda and I have differing views and opinions that still exist today after forty years together. When I wrote *The Relationship Handbook* twenty-five years ago, I believed that those differences of opinion would disappear at some point. I was wrong!

I can say that I now appreciate our differences. I like that Linda sees things differently from me. I have learned to appreciate her views and opinions, and I have even found myself to be influenced by her different ways of looking at things.

In the past when we didn't appreciate our differences, they would rear their contentious heads in almost every discussion we had. When the differences were very fundamental, they seemed to apply to any discussions. For example, every discussion Linda and I had about our kids would really boil down to our different opinions in what children needed. I believed children needed freedom, while Linda believed they needed structure. We argued about this endlessly under different contexts. Sometimes it was about setting a specific bedtime, other times it was about discipline methods. It seemed to us that every discussion was on a totally different topic, when, in reality, we were just arguing about the same basic idea over and over again.

THE MESSY HOUSE CONVERSATION

George. I don't see why you have to put so much pressure on the kids to keep the living room neat. I don't think it's such a big deal that they leave their stuff around.

Linda. It's not a big deal to you because you don't even notice the mess. But it matters to me. I don't see why you don't expect the kids to take care of their stuff.

George. It takes away from their fun. When kids are little they like to space out and enjoy themselves. It's a hassle for them to be told what to do when they don't really understand.

Linda. I'm the one that ends up picking up the mess, not you. Seems to me that you're spoiling the kids letting them live life with no responsibilities and no boundaries.

George. At some point they'll end up doing a lot of things they don't want to do. Why force that on them now?

Linda. I don't want to spoil them, and I don't like a messy house.

George. I'm more interested in their quality of life than I am in how neat the house is. I think you're being a little heavy-handed.

Linda. Well, I think you're being too permissive, and I don't think that's good for us or the kids.

I'm pretty sure that most every reader will identify with one or the other of our positions. Most couples have an authoritarian versus permissive conflict of opinion, and that's okay. The problem in the above dialogue is that it didn't go anywhere, and it wasn't destined to go anywhere. There was no progress or resolution.

Linda's next comment completely turned the discussion in a productive direction. It showed us how we could deal with differing opinions while still coming to some kind of resolution.

Linda. Am I too concerned about spoiling the kids? Don't you think there's a downside to protecting them from the demands of life?

George. I never really thought of the issue of spoiling them in this context. I think you're right that protecting them could spoil them. However, when I look at them I don't see that they are getting spoiled. They seem grateful for what we do for them and for the nice family life we have. Do you think they are getting spoiled?

Linda. Now that you mention it, I don't. I'm just concerned that they will get spoiled if we continue to treat them in, what I would call, a permissive way.

George. If they do start to get spoiled, we can address that then. We are on the same page about that.

Linda. Okay. That helped me with my fear of spoiling them. But I do think that taking on responsibilities is intrinsically good for their upbringing. Do you agree with that?

George. In theory, I do. I just don't want to impose on their sense of freedom in their lives.

Linda. I'm with you on that. I see kids who are suffocated by their parents' demands. I see kids who can't think for themselves because their parents are always telling them what to do. If I felt we were imposing on them too much, I would want to back off. Do you think we are imposing on them too much asking them to keep the common rooms neat?

George. I don't think it would be imposing on them. It would be good for them to contribute, and I know it matters to you. My only reservation is, I don't want your occasional craziness about neatness to set the standard for the family.

Linda. I know what you mean. I'll keep that in check. I will have to, because you're too crazy in the direction of chaos.

George. I can't argue with you there!

This second dialogue was about life. It was about the nature of spoiling kids. It was about the virtues of giving children responsibilities. It was about allowing kids to be kids and balancing that with other priorities. We were able to see that we were philosophically on the same page about those issues, and once we did that, our discussion became very productive.

Not only were these high-level discussions productive, but they were also educational and informative. We both gained a deeper understanding of what "spoiled" meant to each of us. I gained a deeper respect for giving kids an opportunity to contribute. We were humbled by the fact that our "craziness" could contaminate our otherwise good judgment. It did something for both of us that we were on the same page philosophically. It felt like a safety net.

Anytime we get the feeling of déjà vu in our discussions, anytime discussions get unproductive and tight, we ask ourselves: "What is the real, deeper issue in this case? What is the true heart of the matter? And where do each of us stand in that regard?" Just looking in that direction results in us having a productive conversation.

LINDA'S TAKE

Having productive conversations is easy if both people are in a nice feeling. When people aren't upset, they have their bearings. They can listen. They can think intelligently. They can have productive conversations.

When people become upset, they lose their bearings. Their ability to listen well takes a deep dive, and they have trouble thinking productively. It's that simple.

Most people know this already. Where people get into trouble is when they shift into an emotional reaction during a conversation and don't know how to get out of it. The conversation falls apart, and both people are left feeling upset and hopeless—a very bad recipe for productivity.

GETTING OFF THE TRAIN

I once had a client who had a lot of difficulty with talking to her husband about money. She would say things out of anger that would bring down the conversation. She told me that she would think to herself, "You know better than this. Just stop talking." But no matter how hard she tried, she couldn't. She said that she could see when it happened. She could find the exact spot the feeling started going south. And she could see exactly when she should have stepped away from the conversation to let herself cool off. But in the moment of a heated discussion it felt like she was on a train that she just couldn't get off of. She followed the bad feeling hoping to still reach a positive resolution, despite her negativity.

Finally after enough failed attempts, she was convinced in her heart of hearts it was never going to happen. She was never going to be able to solve anything with her husband if she was in a bad feeling. When she let go of trying to make it happen, it allowed her to get off the train and walk away as soon as the conversation started going downhill.

    No one is ultimately stuck in one mindset or one negative feeling. It is possible to leave a conversation and wait for a better feeling in which to return to the conversation. That better feeling can come in a second or maybe longer, but no matter what, it will come.
    This is great because it means that no topics are off limits. Even topics that feel tough, topics that when discussed seem to always end in a fight, become easier to have a conversation about when you wait for the feeling to be right.

THE BIG PICTURE

Betsy and John have been together for two years. Everything has been wonderful between them until recently when things suddenly became difficult. John says he is no longer content with Betsy's kids from a previous relationship. He says that the kids are too needy, dependent and exhausting.

John. This is not what I signed up for.

Betsy. You knew I had kids, and you said you liked kids. All of the sudden the kids are a problem. That doesn't seem fair to me, and it doesn't seem fair to them. They've grown quite attached to you.

John. Well it's been tough. I love you to death, so I was prepared to do what it takes. Now I'm not so sure.

Linda. You two are in a really bad place about this, aren't you?

John. That's an understatement. We talk about the kids until we are blue in the face.

Betsy. I was hoping we could work something out, but every discussion makes it worse. That's why we came to you.

Linda. If every discussion is making it worse, then you aren't having the right kind of discussions.

George. There are ways of discussing things that work for all human beings, and then there are ways that don't work for anyone.

Linda. Sometimes human beings' discussions are philosophical. By that I mean they talk fundamentally, about concepts rather than specific issues. The discussions are more neutral and open-minded. Does this make sense?

Betsy. I know what you mean, but I don't think that's realistic when you're dealing with real life.

Linda. Let's say that right now we are envisioning an ideal world. We want to think about the issue from enough distance that our emotions aren't clouding our minds and, therefore, our discussions.

John. I don't see how we can do that. We need to solve the problem first before we can focus on getting any distance from it. Help us figure out how to make the kids less demanding. They use up all of our energy so Betsy and I have no time to focus on our relationship.

Linda. For now, let's forget about your specific fears and concerns. Instead, we're going to look at the big picture. John, would you say that you care about what matters to Betsy?

John. It's not that simple.

George. You're trying to go back into the world of your problems. Does it ultimately matter to you what matters to Betsy? Is her happiness a concern to you?

John. Of course it is. I've suffered over the fact that she's been so unhappy.

George. Betsy, does it bother you if the kids are problematic to John?

Betsy. Of course. I couldn't overstate how much it matters to me that John feels good about being with my kids. I don't want him to just grin and bear it. I want this to be a joy for him.

John. It really means a lot to me that you care so much. I thought it was all about you and the kids.

Betsy. Of course I care. I love you, and I want to be with you. But I want your being with me to be a plus, not some kind of ordeal. I think a lot of the problem has been that we are both walking around on eggshells, afraid our life together is all going to fall apart.

George. Feeling tense is no fun. When your thoughts pressure you like that, it takes the joy out of life.

John. Believe it or not, it doesn't look like that difficult of a situation to me right at this moment. We love each other. We both love the kids. We both want to make a go of it. All of the issues I had with the kids don't even feel like negatives anymore. I don't even know why it's been so hard.

Linda. George and I have been together for forty years. We love our work. We have wonderful family and friends, and yet sometimes we feel bad about our lives and each other. The only difference is usually we see those bad times as just temporary aberrations, and we don't believe in the hopelessness that we feel. Whatever specific negatives we were hyper-focused on become small concerns that we can easily solve or forget about.

Betsy. But how do you get out of the bad state? That's what I want to learn.

Linda. Just like what you two just did, we look to what ultimately matters. Through your big-picture discussion you both were able to see past the day-to-day reactions, upsets and concerns about the kids, to the fact that loving each other and working things out as partners will always prevail. Now that your heads are in a better place, how do you feel about your situation?

John. I'm realizing that up to now I've just been putting up with the kids, wishing that it was just me and Betsy. I have to take my relationship with them more seriously. I want them to be a plus rather than a minus.

Betsy. For my part, I can stop worrying that things won't work out and put some energy into making things easier for you and the kids. I have put very little into our family lately, because all my thoughts and feelings were tied up in the struggle. I know I could contribute a lot more. I'm sorry I've been so unhelpful.

John. I'm sorry I've been so critical.

Betsy. I would love to bottle up what we found here and bring it home! (Laughs.)

George. The bad news is, you can't put it in a bottle. The good news is that all this hope, all these beautiful feelings, all these great insights are within you. You don't need to pull them out whenever you need to discuss something difficult; they can be a part of your life always.

5
GOOD LISTENING
THE OVERLOOKED RELATIONSHIP SKILL

"My partner says I'm a horrible listener. What am I doing wrong?"

GEORGE'S TAKE

The most commonly used test for a good listener is if the person can repeat back what was said after listening. I have a different test. I ask, "Were you able to hear something *new* in what was being said?" I define listening this way because it supports relationship health.

Poor listening is one of the top reasons couples come to Linda and I for help. Couples complain that their partners don't understand them and that when they do understand, they don't take it to heart. I feel that there is another problem affecting the relationship as well. Poor listening is, by my definition, the reason people get bored with their partners. Good listening keeps partners interested in each other.

THE BAD LISTENER AND THE GOOD LISTENER

I was at a party one day and was talking to a long-time Seattle Seahawks football team season ticket holder. He told me that he was no longer going to games. I was shocked. This was a man who had been so obsessed with the Seahawks, he would wear an elaborate costume to each game. I assumed that he had become bored after watching so many seasons.

I quickly found out that my speculation was wrong when he said, "I love the games, but I can't stand the traffic."

I then made up in my head that he must get bored driving an hour-and-a-half each way for each game. I was wrong again! He told me, "I just can't stand the stress and the road rage."

I was done guessing, but I was curious about why his frustration was so great that he stopped going to games. I asked, "Why does the traffic take such a toll on you? I would have thought you would have gotten use to it by now."

He replied, "It's the stupidity of all the drivers. They change lanes when they shouldn't. They tailgate too much. They swerve."

I had trouble relating to his frustration, but it was interesting to me that his emotional reactions to people's driving mistakes were the reason he didn't go to games.

You will notice that in the story, I listened in two different ways. During the first part of the conversation, I wasn't a good listener. I made a lot of assumptions about my friend. I told myself what he was saying rather than listening directly. During the second part of the conversation, I was a much better listener. I was actually curious to hear what he had to say. I didn't assume why he said the things he did, and I asked questions to find out what he meant when I was confused.

LISTENING TO KEEP THINGS INTERESTING

It has been my observation that the couples who have recently fallen in love are often the most curious about how their partners see the world. They frequently ask the question, "Why do you feel that way?", or say, "Tell me more about that." The curiosity and interest is what keeps the relationship fresh and interesting.

Couples commonly revert to the 'bad listener model' when they talk to each other. They project their own thinking on each other and don't even notice that they are doing it. They just fill in the blanks and assume the other person thinks the way they would think under those circumstances. If they do this often, they lose curiosity for the unique ways their partner actually sees the world.

Linda and I fortunately got on a good roll early on in our relationship. We are like a couple of anthropologists exploring each other's culture. We've been together forty years and yet continue to plow new ground, still gaining new understandings of each other by really listening to each other.

When a couple sees listening as an opportunity to get into another person's world, there is more clarity in the relationship, fewer misunderstandings and more interest and excitement between partners. It feels nice to be heard, but it can feel just as nice to listen.

LINDA'S TAKE

Good listening goes hand-in-hand with good communication. When I say good listening, I don't mean that one person talks while the other person waits for their turn to respond; I mean that each person gets affected by what the other person says and really *sees* their partner's reality.

OUR STORY

George was not always good at listening, especially when we first got together. It was difficult for me to talk to him about it because whenever I would accuse George of not listening to me, he would recite back to me exactly what I had said. This was confusing because he surely was listening if he could do this, but it still didn't feel right. It didn't feel like he was being affected by what I was saying.

It was when George really started to listen, not just hear, but *take in* what I was saying, that I felt a change in our conversations and our relationship. He *felt* what I said, and he was affected by it. He'd tell me that he hadn't realized how I'd felt or how much something mattered to me. It was hard for me not to give him the old eye roll. I must confess that I did often enough! And he would do the same when something he'd been trying to tell me finally hit home.

LISTENING AND COMPASSION

Perhaps one of the most effective tests for if you are a good listener is if you feel compassion for the person you are listening to. Compassion is when your heart goes out to the speaker. Reciting back what someone has said proves that you heard it but not that you felt it. Having compassion proves that you are taking in what someone is saying and that you are allowing it to affect you. I find that compassion is healing. It erases what 'has been'. If what 'has been' is a fight or a heated argument, compassion erases the hurt and anger. If what 'has been' is resentment from a misunderstanding, compassion erases it. Compassion is a cure for grudges. Compassion is a powerful feeling, and it helps relationships move in a positive direction. And it comes quite naturally when people truly listen to each other.

THE THERAPEUTIC POWER OF LISTENING
GEORGE'S STORY

One day I was sitting on a train traveling from Miami to New York, seated next to a sixty-five-year-old gentleman from Richmond, Virginia. I didn't really want the company, and I hoped I could just sit there in silence and observe the scenery, but that was not to be. This man had no shortage of opinions, and he was a storyteller.

He talked about his recent divorce in great detail. He talked about noticing the prejudice that some people had, and he freely admitted to his own prejudice. He talked about how "crazy liberals" were ruining the country, if not the world.

Needless to say, most of what he said was in direct opposition to my own views and beliefs. I was not tempted to take issue with anything, because I didn't want to engage the man further. I asked a few questions to clarify what I didn't understand, but otherwise I stayed quiet.

When the man got to talking about his previous marriage, he became bitter. I could see how difficult his marriage had been and how angry he had become. It was interesting to listen to someone's marital problems without having the responsibility of being their counselor. I felt a lot of compassion for this man's pain. I knew what it was like to feel badly about someone and even be tormented by those feelings. It was easy and natural for my heart to go out to him.

I listened to him talk for over ten hours. I must admit that it was a positive experience because my understanding and compassion for him gave me good feelings. Surprisingly, the experience also had an effect on the man. It had the unintended consequence of requiring him to go back to the drawing board and understand things better for himself.

Bear in mind that there were no interventions on my part. The changes in him came solely from the power of listening. For example, his early thoughts about his ex-wife were, "Our marriage problems were all her fault."

When we got to Washington D.C., he was saying, "I suppose you could say I had some part in our difficulties."

By Philadelphia, he actually said, "Sometimes I feel a certain fondness for Elizabeth. We did have some really good times, but then we screwed it up. It was like we went through the wars, and we were in a foxhole together." I could feel the love he had for his ex-wife, even though he might have denied it.

I saw similar change in his bigotry. He went from blaming everybody but himself, to admitting that the problems of the world were daunting. He respected that there were no easy answers. He even said that there was some merit to liberal ideas, and, believe it or not, he admitted he saw that not everyone was on a level playing field.

His voice was softer and more full of humanness and feeling when we arrived in New York. He was displaying a kinder, more introspective, more humble view of things. He commented that I was an excellent "therapist" (he had previously asked me what I did for a living), even though I offered zero interventions. He did me an equal service. He showed me the therapeutic power of listening with compassion.

6
CAN YOU BE HAPPY WITH ANYONE?

"Sometimes I wonder if I just picked the wrong person. There's got to be someone out there that I'm more compatible with."

GEORGE'S TAKE

My mom was the kind of person who liked everybody and honestly thought everyone was a wonderful person. She thought this was how all people saw each other, and she was puzzled when people viewed others in a negative light.

She often said the phrase, "they mean well." I heard it millions of times from her in response to my dad's criticism of people. She had no idea that she was seeing humanity in a very profound way. It was just natural for her to look past peoples' difficult behaviors and see the goodness in them.

If you buy into my mother's premise that we all have this inherent goodness within us, then the question 'Can you be happy with anyone?' must be answered in the affirmative. Obviously, if you can see and appreciate the beauty, value and goodness of another person on an ongoing basis, you will be happy being in a relationship with them.

I have spent my entire career working with people and learning from them. I truly believe that below our personalities, below our frailties, below our behavioral patterns and below our coping mechanisms, every person on earth has the goodness I spoke of above. Sometimes it is just hard to see.

Is there any evidence for what I'm contending? I would say so:

Everybody sees the goodness in young children, no matter how difficult their behavior. If a child is acting out, an adult will look at them and attempt to understand why. They will wonder if the child is hungry, or tired, or needs attention. The adult will not blame the child for their behavior, but will see the innocence and goodness that exists behind their actions.

When I was in officer training in the army, they taught us that disputes between combatants could be easily turned around by having the combatants clean the opposite sides of the glass windows in the barracks. The combatants could see each other through the glass, but they couldn't talk to each other. In a relatively short time, the combatants were feeling warmly towards each other and even enjoying each other's company in silence. The window made it easy for them to see the humanity in each other rather than their different personalities and frailties.

YOUR PARTNER IS NOT THEIR FRAILTIES

One of the first things that Linda and I teach couples is to turn their attention away from each other's frailties and instead focus on the goodness and humanity that is in each of them. It requires them to step back and look at the nature of life rather than look at the nature of their relationship.

Now you may still be asking yourself, "Why should I allow myself to look past my partner's frailties? Shouldn't they be held responsible for their flaws?" The simple answer is that you desire to have a good relationship with your partner, and therefore you already desire to see the good in them. When you see the good and innocence in another human being, you realize that whatever frailties they have are not as devastating to the relationship as it had looked like before. You can be happy with your partner, not in spite of their frailties, but independent from them.

It can help to understand that your partner *is not* their frailties. When people get caught up in their thinking and become upset, they all have one thing in common: unresponsive, if not dysfunctional, coping mechanisms. Just as a person slipping on ice will contort their body in strange ways to regain their balance, the person emotionally off-balance will behave in puzzling ways in an attempt to regain their emotional bearings. Some people lash out, some become sad, others shut down emotionally. Those behaviors don't make sense to others, except when they know that the person is desperately attempting to regain their emotional bearings and well-being.

If you see that your partner is in a temporary state of insecurity, you will feel compassion. Instead of judging their behavior, you will feel warmly towards them. You will see the inherent goodness in them and in yourself. This alone can get a troubled relationship on good footing.

Can you be happy with anyone? Absolutely, if you can see the inner beauty and goodness that lies within your partner. Doing so will neutralize any frailties the two of you have. Those frailties will even become endearing, just as we find quirky, or even annoying characters in a sitcom endearing.

LINDA'S TAKE

The amount of time spent judging and analyzing your partner, or your emotional reactions to them, is going to undermine your happiness. Some couples find it difficult when they have been together awhile and the rose-colored glasses start to fade. They see flaws in their partner they hadn't noticed before, and they react to them. Their minds recoil, and they think, "Oh no, this is unacceptable. I can't be with a person who is like this!" They fall out of the feeling of love temporarily.

All relationships have these moments of judgment. It's normal. Just like you aren't always going to think that your friend is the world's best friend, you won't always think your partner is the world's best partner.

It becomes a problem if you validate your negative feelings by believing that they must mean something. This makes them stick, and this is where the spiral down to unhappiness begins.

Your next thought might be, "I need to find someone that I can be truly happy with, someone that I am compatible with." The truth is that even the most compatible couples have reactions to each other.

You see, the reactivity, in and of itself, is not the problem. The problem is how serious and important you see your reaction as being, how much time you spend ruminating over it and how much you blame your partner for it. All of this erodes your happiness. It's not that you can't have a meeting of the minds about what is troublesome. You can. And it's not that you have lost your happiness forever. It's just that your mind has switched to dissatisfied mode, and it will switch back.

THE REACTION SPIRAL

I once had a couple come in for counseling who were at the end of their rope, so to speak. The wife was angry about her husband's insensitive behaviors. She told me that he would forget to take out the garbage. He would become distracted when she was telling him a story. He would forget about her diet restrictions when making dinner. The husband felt highly insulted that his wife would treat him the way she did when she got angry. He would become very defensive and closed-off, and this would cause her anger to escalate. They would spend hours trying to have a productive conversation, but each attempt ended in cold silence. They had lost their happiness and felt that they couldn't find it again with the person they were with. They both wanted out of the relationship.

The answer for them was so simple and obvious, yet so obscure. In reactionary states, people don't think straight, and they lose their common sense and perspective. When people have goodwill, they can naturally think straight. They can see what makes sense and what to do.

There is something that brought this couple together, that made them want to have a life together. I showed them that this something was always available to them.

We taught her that her expectations were not some objective truth of how things should be. This understanding allowed her to see that her way of thinking was just one way of seeing relationships. She started to feel less entitled to her way, and as a result, her reactions to her husband softened. We taught her husband how to be less defensive and closed-minded so that he could listen better. When he was able to listen better, he was surprised by how much easier it was for him to talk to his wife. He found that his wife had some pretty good ideas. As a result of all of these shifts in understanding, this couple became very hopeful about their relationship.

THE COMPATIBILITY MYTH

Yes, you can be happy with anyone, because there isn't such thing as an incompatible couple. Being happy with someone does not come from finding the ideal mate for you, but from you being able to hold on to your goodwill and not focusing your mental energy on dissatisfaction and judgments. And when you do have those thoughts, remember that it's just your way of being sometimes. It doesn't mean anything. You can easily bounce back and regain your goodwill and perspective.

DESPERATELY SEEKING

Jen is a twenty-eight-year-old single woman looking for a mate. She just ended a three-year-long relationship. She came to us because she feels she has lost hope in finding the right man.

Jen. I'm beginning to think I'm meant to be alone.

Linda. It may be that you're just not looking at it right. Tell us how you've been going about looking for a mate.

Jen. Well, I've been in three serious relationships as well as several other short-term ones. I have a pretty good idea of what I'm looking for. I also don't think I'm being unrealistic in what I'm looking for. I'm just tired of looking and tired of being disappointed.

Linda. You said you have a pretty good idea of what you're looking for. Can you say more about that?

Jen. I have a list of deal breakers.

Linda. Could I assume that the list of requirements and deal breakers has gotten longer over time?

Jen. It has. I have become increasingly more discriminating because I don't want to waste time on relationships that I know won't work for me.

George. Can I share an idea with you that may seem ridiculous?

Jen. I'm open to anything that might help.

George. I think it's a mistake to look at people's personalities when in the pursuit of a mate. If you could look beyond people's personalities to their true nature, you would see possibility in everyone. The pool of possible mates would be considerably larger than the pool you have made for yourself with your deal breakers and requirements.

Jen. Are you saying that I should just pick someone at random?

Linda. We are suggesting that if a couple is not happy, it's because they haven't been able to see past personality incompatibility issues to appreciate the true essence of the other person.

Jen. It is a stretch for me to believe that any two people could not only get along but even find love for each other.

Linda. Imagine that two strangers jumped from a shipwreck into an unstable lifeboat. Imagine that they spent weeks navigating the boat in search of land. They find an isolated island and work together to stay alive. Don't you think that these two people would grow fond of each other and find a connection beyond their personalities? Don't you think that, out of necessity, they would learn to take each other's personality traits in stride and even find them endearing at times?

Jen. I don't know that I could do that with my ex-boyfriends. (Smiles.)

George. They say that necessity is the mother of invention. If conditions were as demanding as the ones described, I don't think you would afford yourself the luxury of indulging your reactions and judgments about the other person. When people connect on a human level, their reactions and their judgments fade into the background.

Jan. I find this discussion disconcerting. You're basically telling me to select a mate by throwing a dart at the phone book.

Linda. We are not telling you how to select a mate. We are suggesting that thinking about your criteria and making sure that people meet that criteria is creating bad feelings that you are attributing to the person you're dating. Keeping your mind open and enjoying yourself with your date would allow you to feel closer to the person you're with. It would open you up to more possibility.

George. If you had an enjoyable experience for each person you dated, the dating process would be hopeful rather than tense and disappointing.

Jen. If I liked every person I dated, how would I know how to pick?

Linda. You would see where the relationships lead. At some point you would have the thought, "This is the person I want to be with."

Jen. That seems like a tall order.

George. You face the same options once you are in a relationship with the person of your choice. If you fill your head with judgments, concern and evaluations of your partner, then you will not be able to fully enjoy the relationship. If you enjoy the person despite his supposed shortcomings, then you will live in that feeling of happiness.

Jen. I see that I was off track.

Linda. That is no problem. Everyone seems to believe that there are only a few paths to happiness, when in reality, you can find happiness in any circumstance or partner, if you keep an open mind.

7
FINAL THOUGHTS

Love is so close to the surface that it can suddenly and predictably appear even in the midst of negative feelings. Love is at our core. Scratch the surface of our persona, our personality, our thinking, and you touch our humanity. We experience it whenever we have a warm, joyful feeling.

It is infinitely more realistic for an unhappy couple to meet at their humanity than it is to try to work out their personality differences and the problems that arose from those differences. Knowing that our core of love is the constant among us human beings makes it easy to be hopeful in hard times and to be faithful when our resolution efforts have failed us. When we work with couples, we point them away from personal differences and personal thought-systems, because we know no answers exist in that direction. Instead, we point them towards the common humanity and love that is their nature.

If we have love and connectedness at our core, then why is the divorce rate so high? It certainly wouldn't be an understatement to say that for centuries human beings have been underachievers in the relationship arena. Here is the problem: we all have the free will to do things as we see fit. In the moment, our thinking looks real and compelling to us. If our thinking is at odds with our mate, we focus on resolving our differences and end up moving farther away from our natural connectedness. As we stray from those feelings of love and closeness, we feel lonely and misunderstood.

No matter how far down the rabbit hole the couple travels, they are only one thought away from feeling the love that is at their core. As soon as love appears, they have all the feelings they need to support a healthy relationship, no matter the challenges. When you put pure light through a prism, you see the colors of the rainbow appear. The prism adds nothing to the light. The rainbow simply exhibits the aspects of light.

When pure love goes through the prism that is a human being, it manifests a variety of life-enhancing feelings, such as compassion, humility, affinity and closeness. These feelings are the foundation of sustainable human relationships. You are only required to look beyond the appearance of personality and behavior, to the true essence of your partner, and yourself.

ADDITIONAL RESOURCES

For more of the learning found in this book, consider the resources listed below. All are available in the store at **www.pranskyandassociates.com**.

AUDIO PRODUCTS

The Pransky and Associates audio collection consists of more than fifty titles, including:

- Maintenance-Free Relationships: *How to Improve Your Relationship without 'Working on It'*

- Mental Traction Factor: *The Power to have Productive Conversations even when the Subject is Sensitive and the Participants Defensive*

- Relationship Quicksand: *Four Things we're Taught to do in our Relationships that don't Work*

ONLINE COURSE

INSIGHT for Relationships: More Ups, Less Downs

This is an in-depth online course based on the approach found in *The Relationship Handbook*. As one of the co-creators, Dr. George Pransky spent over two years developing this course to be a comprehensive foundation for relationships.

SOURCE MATERIAL BY SYDNEY BANKS

The discoveries of Sydney Banks are the basis for this book. If you are interested in the origins and source of the logic presented here, Sydney Banks' books, CDs and DVDs provide the clearest and deepest expression of that logic.

CREDITS

TRANSLATIONS COORDINATOR
Véronique Pivetta

FRENCH TRANSLATION
Translators: Martine Etienne, Véronique Pivetta
Editors: Jasmyne DesBiens, Sandie Martel

DUTCH TRANSLATION
Translator: Véronique Pivetta
Editors: Kelly Van Hecke, Maria Stuer

NORWEGIAN TRANSLATION
Translators: Pål Davik, Kaja Flatøy
Editors: Anita Grøsland, Eirik Grunde Olsen, Klaus Pettersen

SWEDISH TRANSLATION
Translator: Marita Forsvid Lund
Editors: David Andersson, Tina Hedberg, Thomas Lund

GERMAN TRANSLATION
Translator: Agnetha Henne
Editors: Justyna Rutkowski, Katja Symons, Daniela Tettamanti

SPANISH TRANSLATION
Translators: Lina Garcia, Véronique Pivetta
Editors: Angus Alvarez

Printed in Great Britain
by Amazon